KV-435-651

Problem Solving Interviews

Problem Solving Interviews

W. E. BEVERIDGE

London
GEORGE ALLEN & UNWIN LTD
RUSKIN HOUSE · MUSEUM STREET

FIRST PUBLISHED IN 1968
SECOND IMPRESSION 1973

This book is copyright under the Berne Convention. All rights are reserved. Apart from any fair dealing for the purpose of private study, research, criticism or review, as permitted under the Copyright Act, 1956, no part of this publication may be reproduced, stored in a retrieval system, or transmitted, in any form or by any means, electronic, electrical, chemical, mechanical, optical, photocopying, recording or otherwise, without the prior permission of the copyright owner. Enquiries should be addressed to the publishers.

© George Allen & Unwin Ltd, 1968

ISBN 0 04 137004 X

CITY OF BIRMINGHAM
POLYTECHNIC LIBRARY

BOOK
No.   070313

SUBJECT
No.   158.3

PRINTED IN GREAT BRITAIN BY
REDWOOD PRESS LIMITED
TROWBRIDGE, WILTSHIRE

Contents

Contents

CHAPTER ONE

The Role of the Problem-solving Interviewer

There are a great many people—managers, supervisors, doctors, nurses, schoolteachers, personnel officers, welfare workers, clergymen and the like—who spend a considerable part of their working time simply talking with people. They are not usually engaged in small talk but are concerned with some situation which presents them with a problem and demands the making of a decision about the best way to solve it. This kind of talk amounts to one form of the interview and the role relationship between the two talkers is that of 'interviewer' and 'respondent'. The conversation between them may have been initiated either by the interviewer or the respondent on the ground that the latter needs help in defining his problem and deciding how it can best be solved. This means that the interviewer must help the respondent to accomplish two tasks; first to clarify the facts so that he can see precisely what his problem is, and secondly to clarify his attitudes towards the problem situation so that he is enabled to take these into account when he comes to make his decision about how to solve it.

The problem-solving interviewer will not usually see himself as a counsellor, although the demarcation line that separates him from the counsellor cannot be defined too precisely and counsellors regularly engage in problem-solving interviews as part of their work. In helping the respondent to solve his problem, the interviewer enables him also to see himself in a new perspective, to understand himself more clearly,

9

to become aware of his attitudes and take account of them in a new way, but the interviewer's chief concern will be simply to enable the respondent to solve a particular problem, not to come to terms with himself as a person.

The therapeutic counsellor is concerned primarily with the integration of the person who has the problem; the problem-solving interviewer is concerned primarily that a particular person be helped to solve a particular problem. Of course the counsellor will be concerned with the problem and the interviewer with the person; the difference between them is a matter of emphasis. This emphasis will however determine the shape and style of the interaction between the two people. The counsellor will be likely to meet his client again and again; he will be deeply concerned with unconscious attitudes and motivation and with the client's behaviour over a whole range of situations. The problem-solving interviewer will meet the respondent once or twice; he will be primarily concerned with eliciting facts, with the respondent's consciously accepted attitudes and with helping to clarify a particular situation so that the respondent may deal with it more effectively. This type of interview is normally concerned with situational problems in which a decision has to be made about what action is appropriate, such action to be taken within a limited period of time.

For example, a manager invites his training officer to discuss how he feels about a new training scheme that has recently been set up in the company with a view to making decisions about future training needs. A young and aggrieved secretary hands in her notice to her manager who interviews her about her reasons for deciding to leave the company so that she may clarify her thinking and be able to make a more informed decision. A personnel manager interviews a colleague whose hopes of taking a higher level position in Scotland have been dashed by his wife's unwillingness to leave London and who is uncertain what to do. A full-time social worker, who is having difficulty in getting adequate service from her voluntary staff, is interviewed in an attempt to help her make an appropriate decision about what action she might take to resolve this awkward situation. We shall be looking at each of these interview situations in the course of the book. In none of them is a long drawn out counselling procedure called for nor a complete reorientation of the respondent's personality. The respondent is not 'sick' and in need of therapy; he is a normal human being, sometimes frustrated, sometimes immature emotionally but not always so, who needs wise and skilled help so that he may handle some particular problem adequately.

The exercise of such short-term help is the objective of the problem-solving interviewer. It is not his task to undertake a long-term analysis of the respondent's *ego* with a view to enabling him reshape his attitudes to life and integrate his personality. He does not set out to enter into a lengthy relationship with him in which he can develop a new degree of psychological self-awareness. His role is supportive; he stands alongside the respondent while he deals with his problem. For help other than this—for example, long-term relationships in which an emotionally deprived individual experiences the closeness and confidence which enable him eventually to function successfully and independently in his total life situation—the respondent must turn elsewhere. But this limited help is all that many people need, the help of a wise and understanding fellow human-being whose skill will enable them to clarify a particular situation and come to an appropriate decision about it. This help, limited and short-term as it may be, calls not only for considerable interviewing skill on the part of the interviewer but also for an understanding of attitudes and the way in which they affect a person's 'perception' of his situation. Indeed the very fact that it is short-term makes special demands on the interviewer in ensuring that he focuses the interview on the particular situation and does not allow the respondent to lead him into an examination of his problems in general.

Many people who would certainly not think of their work as primarily that of interviewing nevertheless find themselves engaged in conducting interviews from time to time, enquiring of other people what their attitudes are to this particular situation or to that, why they are distressed about this problem or that, helping them to make up their minds about appropriate decisions to take. It is all too easy sometimes to refer such interviews to the trained specialist—the medical social worker or the marriage guidance counsellor or the personnel manager. There are indeed interviews that need such referral but there are many which are more properly carried out by the supervisor or the ward sister or the departmental manager or the schoolteacher partly because this may be more acceptable to the respondent—he may wish to talk with someone he knows already and with whom he is in regular contact—and partly because the supervisor or ward sister or departmental manager or schoolteacher concerned has a role responsibility towards the respondent. For example, the industrial supervisor has a responsibility towards an operator just because he is his supervisor and he ought not to try to pass this responsibility on to the personnel manager unless he has good grounds for believing that the kind of help the operator needs is more than he is equipped to give. It is not being suggested that managers, ward sisters, supervisors, schoolteachers and the like should be equipped to act as counsellors but simply that they ought to be able to handle more adequately than many of them at the moment are able to do some of the problems of those with whom they come into contact and who may indeed regard them as the appropriate people to approach when they have problems to deal with.

There are of course some problems which are of such a technical nature that the only person who can help is one who shares the respondent's technical expertise and is thus qualified to ask relevant questions. For example, a supervisor who is concerned about the way in which one of his charge hands is discharging his duties may prefer to have an interview with the departmental manager who is more closely aware of the conditions under which charge hands have to work in his department rather than be referred to a skilled interviewer in the personnel department who is not so closely in touch either with the charge hand concerned or with the conditions under which he has to carry out his job. The departmental manager will not however be able to help him as adequately as he might unless he has some knowledge of the skills of interviewing. Many people have gained an understanding of interviewing techniques through their experience of life and through having had to interview people about their problems over many years. It is in the hope that such people may be helped to deal with their interview situations with a greater degree of skill that this book has been written as well as in the belief that there are many young men and women entering into positions of responsibility in society who would deal with them more effectively if they learned a more systematic approach to the techniques of helping those with whom they come into contact to sort their problems.

To say all this is to imply that there are more jobs for which the knowledge and practice of interviewing skills are important than one might realize at first thought. In fact, it is hard to envisage any job which involves responsibility for working with people and which does not also involve from time to time the need to interview them about some problem connected with themselves or with their work.

CHAPTER TWO

What is an Interview?

When two people enter into a conversation we may ask three questions about it: (1) What is it about? (2) What is its purpose? (3) Does either speaker 'direct' the pattern or shape of the conversation? We may even ask a fourth question: (4) Do the speakers talk about the same amount or does one talk more than the other?

Here are two conversations about which we may ask these three questions and our fourth supplementary one.

I. MR SMITH MEETS MR JONES ON THE BUS

'Ah, good morning, Mr Jones. Haven't seen you for a long time.'

'No indeed. It must be three or four weeks. Have you been out of town?'

'Well, I had to go up north for four days last week. Otherwise I've been around as usual.'

'I expect we've just caught different buses. Such an erratic service they provide. Still seem to use the convoy system.'

'How right you are. I've been tempted more than once to take the car but parking near my office is nearly impossible.'

'Well, I could manage that but my wife likes me to leave it. It's handy for her to take the children to school and do the shopping.'

'Yes, of course. By the way, how is she? Last time we met you said she was a bit under the weather.'

'Oh, the doctor gave her some tablets and she is fine now.

14

Look, you and your wife must come round and have supper with us one evening.'

'Thank you. We'd love to.'

'I'll give you a ring tonight and we'll fix a date.'

'Good.'

FIRST QUESTION: *What is the conversation about?* It is about Mr Smith's absence, the bus service, the difficulties of taking a car to town, Mrs Jones's illness and a supper invitation. The speakers talk about a number of unrelated topics, each of which comes up almost by chance.

SECOND QUESTION: *What is the purpose of the conversation?* It does not have any obvious purpose. At the most, one might say that it is intended to express general friendliness.

THIRD QUESTION: *Does either speaker 'direct' the pattern or shape of the conversation?* Here the answer is clearly no. Mr Smith introduces the topics of his own absence, the difficulties of taking the car to town and Mrs Jones's health. Mr Jones introduces the topics of the erratic bus service and the supper invitation. The conversation moves forward in an undirected fashion.

FOURTH QUESTION: *Do the speakers talk about the same amount or does one talk more than the other?* Both speakers talk about the same amount. Mr Smith uses 80 words; Mr Jones uses 102 words.

II. MR SMITH MEETS MR BROWN IN HIS OFFICE

'Good morning, Mr Brown. Come and sit down.'

'Thank you.'

'I wanted to have a word with you about this new supervisory training programme you have set up. How do you feel it's going?'

15

'Pretty well, thank you, Mr Smith. Of course it's too early yet to make a complete assessment but the supervisors who have been on it all seem enthusiastic.'

'That sounds encouraging. What did they say they specially liked about it?'

'I think the opportunity to sit back and look at their jobs a bit more objectively than usual. And of course the chance to talk with each other about their problems.'

'Any special problems that seemed to bother them?'

'The whole business of communication is one they give a lot of time to. Now that the company has introduced 'briefing sessions' right down from top management to the shop floor, they're specially interested in their own part in all this and of course in particular the 'briefing sessions' they have to conduct with their own operators. They said they had been having a bit of difficulty here but that they find the training we have been giving in running practice sessions has been useful to them.'

'You must be pleased about this.'

'Yes, I am. And we are going to develop this side of the training programme even more.'

FIRST QUESTION: *What is the conversation about?* It is about the training programme. The speakers have one specific topic in mind throughout the whole of their conversation and the conversation is not allowed to drift away from this topic at any point.

SECOND QUESTION: *What is the purpose of the conversation?* It is to enable Mr Smith to discuss with Mr Brown the progress of the training programme so that the latter may make appropriate decisions about his plans for developing it in the future.

THIRD QUESTION: *Does either speaker 'direct' the pattern or shape of the conversation?* Yes, Mr Smith does so. He decides the shape the conversation is to take when he explains its purpose as being to discuss the new training programme and Mr Brown's feelings about its progress. He picks up Mr Brown's remark about the enthusiasm of the supervisors and asks him to enlarge on it. He directs the conversation into the area of problems that may need to be dealt with.

While Mr Smith directs the conversation, he does not attempt to control it precisely. A conversation involves interaction between two people so both contribute to its eventual shape. But Mr Smith gives an outline of the shape he wants it to be; it is to be 'about this new supervisory training programme you have set up. How do you feel it's going?' He picks up points that Mr Brown makes and directs the conversation towards them; this means he has to be flexible, he cannot completely plan the shape of the conversation in advance. But the conversation is directed by his response to Mr Brown's contribution to it.

FOURTH QUESTION: *Do the speakers talk about the same amount or does one talk more than the other?* Mr Brown talks about three times as much as Mr Smith does; he uses 165 words to Mr Smith's 58 words. So while Mr Smith directs the shape of the conversation, he also does most of the listening and Mr Brown most of the talking.

The first conversation is no more than a casual affair, the kind of friendly chat we indulge in every day when we meet people with whom we share few or no common objectives. The second conversation however is an interview. If then we look at the answers to our three main questions, we can obtain a definition of the interview. It is a conversation which has a specific topic (in this case the training programme) and a specific purpose (to discover how it is progressing and to make plans for its development) and the pattern or shape of which is directed by the interviewer (Mr Smith).

17

We may write this out as follows:

An interview is a conversation within a specific context and having a specific purpose, the pattern of which is directed by the interviewer.

The answer to our fourth and subsidiary question informs us also that the interviewer tends to talk less than the respondent and therefore listens more. The interviewer's job is to enable the respondent to talk as freely as possible within the context of the subject matter with which the interview is concerned. This of course places certain limitations on the respondent and makes considerable demands on the skills of the interviewer.

We tend very often to think of an interview as rather a formal event, something which takes place across an office desk and usually between a superior and his or her subordinate. It is the sort of thing people undergo when they have applied for a job or asked for an increase in salary and a manager has asked them into his office to discover why they think they are worth it or even perhaps when they are being called to account for some shortcoming in their work. They are interviewed. In fact, a great many interviews take place without any of these trappings of formality at all. For example, a nursing sister may find herself involved in getting down the details of a patient's medical history; this may be a fairly formal sort of interview. But she may also take part in a conversation with a nervous patient who has come into hospital for an operation and is very frightened. Such a conversation can be just as much an interview as the information-gathering of the first occasion when she obtained the patient's medical history. For it is 'a conversation within a specific context' (it is about the patient's operation and his feelings of distress and fear), 'with a specific purpose' (to help him deal with his situation more constructively by developing a new attitude towards it), 'the pattern of which is directed by the interviewer' (the inter-

viewer asks appropriate questions to draw out the patient's
fears and enable him to look at them and come to terms with
them).

Or again, while he is standing by his machine on the factory
floor, an operator whose wife died a year or two back may
discuss with his supervisor the problem of whether or not he
should give up his home after his impending retirement and go
to live with his married daughter and her family in another part
of London. On the one hand he likes the idea of being with
one of his own kith and kin and he has always been specially
fond of his daughter and she of him. If he were ill, she'd be
able to look after him. On the other hand he is afraid that he
might be a bit of a nuisance to her with being around the
house all day and he is not keen either on losing his indepen-
dence. Then again, he would be away from all his old friends
with whom he has worked for so many years in the factory.
He just does not know what to do and wants to talk it over
with somebody. The conversation can become an interview if
the supervisor refrains from giving dogmatic advice and instead attempts to help the operator think systematically
through his problem so that he can begin to see clearly the
implications of each of the possible courses of action open to
him and decide which one is most acceptable. Once again we
have 'a conversation within a specific context' (it is about the
problem of whether or not the operator should go to live with
his daughter after his retirement), 'with a specific purpose'
(to help the operator think through the alternatives sufficiently carefully to be able to make an acceptable decision), 'the
pattern of which is directed by the interviewer' (the supervisor
decides what areas of the problem need systematic investigation and asks appropriate questions to help the operator think
fully through these).

Both these conversations, though they take place in quite
informal circumstances, are interviews. They are in fact both
problem-solving interviews. In the first, the nurse is helping

the patient to deal with the problem presented by his own fears. In the second, the supervisor is helping the operator deal with the problem of what action to take in a situation in which he is being pulled in two opposite directions. The special characteristics of the problem-solving interview are that it involves a problem situation for the respondent who wants or needs help so that he can see it objectively, envisage some kind of constructive solution to it and make a decision about what action is best to bring this solution about.

Let us take for illustration a conversation which takes place between a personnel officer and his friend and colleague, a departmental manager:

'Good morning, John. I believe you want to see me. Take a seat.'

'Thanks. Yes I do actually. I wanted to have a word with you if you could spare me a quarter of an hour.'

'Of course. What's it all about?'

'The proposed job in Scotland as a matter of fact. I think you know that Robinson has asked me to consider taking over the new factory outside Glasgow. I was pretty delighted when I heard the news. It's to be a fine new building—lots of opportunities—marvellous countryside, an easy car run away—I've always loved Scotland and the idea of living there seemed wonderful.'

'Mm hmm. What's the problem then?'

'Well, it's Dorothy. She's just completely unenthusiastic.'

'You mean she won't go?'

'I wouldn't say that exactly. But she clearly is not very impressed with the idea of leaving London. Of course she has always lived here—she was born and brought up here and went to school here. All her friends are here. Then, as you know, her father died a few months ago and she obviously feels badly about the thought of leaving her mother and younger sister. They've been seeing a lot of each other in recent weeks. Then there's Johnny—he's ten and settled down at last in school; he wasn't happy for a long time. Dorothy is afraid he won't find it easy to be transplanted not only from school but from his home background—the friends he has got down here. I can tell you, Dick, when I got home last night with the great news, as I imagined it, I got rather a poor reception.'

'What did you say to all this?'

'What could I say? I went home bursting with enthusiasm. Dorothy is distressed because she can't be enthusiastic. I think she feels she is letting me down. She looked really upset at breakfast this morning—I'm sure she hadn't slept properly. But I can see her point about her mother—it's a bit hard for her to lose her husband and then have her daughter move miles away to Scotland. They've always been very close to each other and the old man's death has made Dorothy feel her mother is really dependent on her at the moment. Then there's Johnny—I don't want to upset him with it all.'

'Does he know about it?'

'Oh no. I mean, after Dorothy's reaction I thought the best thing was to say nothing.'

'But Dorothy hasn't made up her mind yet?'

'I suppose not. I mean, she's obviously torn two ways. She doesn't want to stand in the way of my getting promotion; she can see the advantages well enough. At the same time she doesn't want to move out of London because of her mother. It's as simple as that.'

'Might your mother-in-law be willing to go up north with you?'

'She wouldn't leave town. Anyway, there's Dorothy's sister—she's unmarried and at business and the mother runs the home for her. The old lady would not want to leave her on her own. As a matter of fact, Dorothy tried to persuade her parents to think about moving down to Sussex when the

21

old man retired. He'd have liked to have gone; he went and looked at quite a number of places. But she was adamant; she wasn't leaving London. And nobody could budge her. Dorothy is like her in lots of ways—I think she feels she would not be happy outside London herself.'

'Mm. Do you think she might feel differently about moving in, say, six months time, when her mother is more adjusted to being on her own?'

'It's hard to say. Frankly, I just would not know. She might agree. I would be quite ready to go into a hotel and come home at weekends for the first six months or so if that helped. In any case, it would be some time before we could sell our present house and buy a new one. But I've to make a decision quickly.'

'How quickly?'

'Well, Robinson told me to go home and talk things over with the family. Of course he has no idea how Dorothy feels. Then he suggested I ought to go up to Glasgow and size up the situation there. So that's bound to take a week or two. But I think he wants an answer pretty quickly. I ought to give him an answer within ten days or so.'

'Mm hmm. And what happens if you say no?'

'What do you mean?'

'How would it affect your position in the company?'

'That's a difficult question to answer. I doubt if they'd offer me another job like this. And there is nothing in the way of promotion within the company likely in the London area. The only hope of promotion really is out of London. And if I say no to this job, I may not get the chance to say no again.'

'So really if you want promotion in this company it looks as if you may have to accept this job.'

'It does, doesn't it? I should have foreseen this situation years ago. It seems likely that either I have to stay at my present level or accept this job if I'm to continue with the company. The only alternative seems to be to look around for a bigger job with another company in the London area or at least a job that offers promotion prospects in London.'

'How would you feel about doing that?'

'Oh, I suppose if the right job turned up it might be the answer. I feel I've got to get promotion pretty soon if I'm to get it at all. That is why this chance seemed so wonderful.'

'I can see that. It raises quite a few family problems for you.'

'Yes, but you can't have everything.'

'You feel you may have to take it in spite of the family.'

'Oh hell. You know I can't do that, Dick. Promotion isn't everything. What kind of life would it be for us if Dorothy was really unhappy? And there is Johnny to consider. I don't want to mess things up for him.'

'So what is your alternative?'

'To turn it down, I suppose. And then to look around for something else. It will be quite a wrench to leave the company —I feel established here. Secure, if you know what I mean. But maybe a change would be good for me. Maybe I'm getting too settled.'

'You feel you're getting into a sort of rut.'

'In a way, I suppose. I'll just have to be a bit more adventurous—really begin to look around. I expect that means I'll have to say no to this job fairly quickly. It would not be fair to waste people's time when I know I can't take it.'

'Mm hmm.'

'I knew all along, I suppose, that it would not be fair to Dorothy to go ahead with this—once I heard her reactions last night. But I think now I've to get down to looking a bit more carefully at my future.'

'You mean, to think about a new job outside the company.'

'Yes, that seems to be the only real answer. There's nothing else I can do if I'm to get a bigger job and still stay around the London area.'

In this conversation, the personnel officer encourages John

to look honestly at his problem and assess all the implications of the alternative decisions he might make about the company's offer of the job in Scotland. John concludes, 'It seems likely that either I have to stay at my present level or accept this job if I'm to continue with the company. The only alternative seems to be to look around for a bigger job with another company in the London area or at least a job that offers promotion prospects in London.' The personnel officer asks how he would feel about leaving the company. John is forced to recognize that he would prefer to stay in the company but that this would mean the end of any hope of promotion. He is pursuing a number of objectives which do not fit together: he wants promotion, to stay with his present company, to live in London because this is important to his wife and family. But he cannot achieve all of these at the same time. The personnel officer's questions help him to recognize this fact and that he must therefore make a decision about which goals are most important to him. Will he stay in the company and take his promotion, thereby endangering his family's happiness? Or will he stay in the company and accept the fact that he must remain at his present level so that his family can stay in London? Or will he move out of the company and look for a bigger job in a new company in London thereby satisfying his desire for promotion and safeguarding his family happiness? The personnel officer does not suggest that one of these courses is any better than another or more worth while. His role is simply to help John reach the point when he can make a decision for himself.

The result of the problem-solving interview is the creation by the respondent of a new and more positive attitude to the problem; to that extent it is therapeutic. This new perception of his problem usually leads to his taking a decision about it: in some cases this may be no more than a decision to accept it without resentment; in others, it may be a decision to take a specific course of action regarding it.

Human decisions are not always based on rational grounds. Feelings count for as much as reason. We do not however always recognize why we make the decisions we do. Very often we think we have decided to do something because this is the most logical course of action when, in fact, the real source of our decisions may be largely emotional. Mr X decides to buy a new car. He tells himself that really his old car is past its best, that if he kept it for another year he would be liable to have to face more and more bills for repairs, that he might have a breakdown while on the holiday he plans to take with his wife next year in Spain and could have it spoiled. So he concludes that in the long run it would be both cheaper and safer to invest in a new car. How much his decision was due to these facts and how much to the facts that Mr Y next door has just bought a new car and Mr X has been regarding it rather enviously and that Mrs Y made a disparaging remark about the X family car to Mrs X last week is not easy to determine. But it is likely that Mr X's decision is not so logical as he thinks it is and that his envy of Mr Y's new car and resentment at Mrs Y's remark to his wife also helped him to make his decision. The problem-solving interview is concerned both with rational and emotional factors, not only with logical thinking but also with attitudes. So it is important for us to look now at the way in which attitudes are built up and how they affect the manner in which we perceive situations and behave in them.

CHAPTER THREE

Attitudes and Behaviour

The foreman of an assembly shop in an engineering firm once told me of the trouble he was having with one of his operators, a coil winder, because of the man's attitude to his work. 'Everything he turns out could be put in an exhibition,' he said. 'The man is a perfectionist. He gets half-way through a coil, then decides it isn't satisfactory and takes it all to pieces. The result is that he seems to spend more time unwinding coils than winding them. I've been at him about production needs but it doesn't seem to make the slightest difference. He is losing bonus too.' In the end the operator had to be moved from the job. The company did not want their coils to be of exhibition standard; they simply wanted coils that were functional—and lots of them. But the operator was not prepared to work to company standards; for him only the best was good enough. So strongly did he hold this perfectionist attitude towards his work that he was prepared to allow the company to lose production and himself to lose bonus and, in the end, his job, rather than change it.

Attitudes are pretty clearly strong and tough and affect not only how we feel about people, things and situations, but also how we behave towards them. We all have attitudes towards race, religion, accent, appearance, the opposite sex, foreigners, work, our superiors, our subordinates, and so on. In the case of the coil winder, his perfectionist attitude affected not only how he felt towards his work but how he did it. In a work situation, attitudes are always important because they affect people's success in doing their work effectively. Selectors of men and women for jobs have to ask themselves, 'Will these people have not only the *capacity* to do this job but the *inclination* as well?' In other words, they have to be concerned not only with whether the candidate for the job can actually perform it adequately, but with how far he will be able to like it or at least find it tolerable. A bright girl may learn how to do an assembly job very quickly. Her supervisor is delighted because in two or three hours she has learned what it takes most girls a week to learn; he thinks he has found an ideal employee. How wrong he is he discovers when, at the end of her first month, the girl hands in her notice. She has become bored with the job because it makes too few demands on her. Other girls who take longer to learn the job because they are not quite so bright tend perhaps to stay much longer. It may be that they are looking for something different in their work situation and so adopt a different attitude to the job from the first girl. The first girl, just because she is bright, may be looking for a job that will make some demands on her intelligence. The other girls, who are not so bright, may be prepared to do a job that the first girl sees only as repetitive, monotonous and dull because they are looking for something different in their work situation—perhaps an easy job that makes few demands on them intellectually but gives them the opportunity to talk freely with other girls during working hours. We say their attitudes towards the job are different; they are perceiving the same job in different ways—the first girl as boring and therefore intolerable, the other girls as easy and giving opportunities for social contact, and therefore pleasant.

Attitudes get tied together to form 'frames of reference' for us. Every one of us perceives the world through his own attitudes and he cannot always easily distinguish in what he perceives between what the world outside gives and what he himself gives to the 'perception'. A 'perception' is really a complex structure partly supplied by the world outside us and partly by our own attitudes to things. We can illustrate this

27

diagrammatically by representing an objective situation as a square ■. When we perceive such a situation, we never get it on its own but always framed around by our attitudes. If we represent two different sets of attitudes by lines surrounding the square, two people may look at the same situation but may 'perceive' different things because they look at a whole picture formed by the combination of the objective situation (the square) within the framework of their own attitudes (the surrounding line). The two different perceptions of the same situation are illustrated in the two figures below.

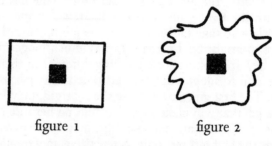

figure 1   figure 2

The objective situation might be a new work method which an industrial manager decides to introduce into the machine shop of his engineering firm. The manager holds favourable attitudes towards efficiency and as he thinks it likely that the new method will improve efficiency by increasing production and lowering costs; he therefore adopts a favourable attitude towards the new method of working. He also holds favourable attitudes towards the possibility of prestige and promotion for himself and, as he thinks it likely the new method will increase his prestige and improve the possibility of his promotion, this adds to the strength of his favourable attitudes to the new method. His 'perception' of the new work method is thus influenced very considerably by his favourable attitudes towards it. Let us take it that what he perceives is represented by figure 1. At this point the manager goes on to introduce the new method and is shocked when he meets resistance from the men on the shop floor. He castigates the shop stewards, who represent the men, for being difficult and obstructionist. What he fails to realize is that they are not perceiving what he perceives because the attitudes with which they surround the new work method are not the same as his own.

The men on the shop floor hold unfavourable attitudes towards loss of earnings and redundancy. Because of past experience they are only too well aware that innovations in work methods have produced both of these unpleasant results for them. They have had no reassurance that this one now proposed will be any different so they at once see it within the context of loss of money and possible redundancy. Their unfavourable attitudes to these factors result in an unfavourable attitude towards the new method, an attitude which we may represent by the wavy line which surrounds the square in figure 2.

This means that the manager and the men are not perceiving the same thing. The manager perceives figure 1; the men figure 2. And not until the manager takes the trouble to discover how the men perceive the new method, to learn what their 'frame of reference' is, can he begin to take steps that may allay their fears.

If someone comes to me with a grievance, it may seem so small and silly as not to be worth bothering about and I may be tempted to dismiss it rather curtly with some such remark as 'Oh, go away and get on with your job.' But if I am concerned not simply with the situation which has given rise to the grievance but also with the person who holds the grievance, I will begin to look for the 'frame of reference' within which he perceives it so that I may take account of this in helping him deal with what he feels as his problem.

A slight rebuke may reduce one girl to tears, inflame another to angry defiance and glide gently off a third. The rebuke is the same in each case; it is the girls who are different. They

29

hold different attitudes and so perceive the rebuke in different ways. The first girl, who breaks into tears, may feel unloved and unwanted. What do I know about her early home life and childhood? What do I know about some traumatic experience she may have had? Is she easily upset because she is unsure of herself and sees every word of criticism as a personal affront? The second girl, who expresses defiance, may feel the world is against her and she must fight it. As with the first girl, I can only help her if I begin to understand the 'frame of reference' within which she perceives the rebuke. The third girl, who remains calm and unruffled, may feel secure and self-assured, able to regard the rebuke as a constructive comment which will help her to do better next time. For her the rebuke does not present a threat. Here we have an instance of the same situation presenting itself as a problem to two girls but not to the third. It is clear that the rebuke on its own does not create the problem situation but the rebuke within the context of the girls' attitudes. The first girl possesses an insecure attitude to life, the second an aggressive one. It is their attitudes that make them perceive the rebuke as a threat and to become people with problems. The third girl is saved because her attitude towards her environment, including the rebuke, is a confident one. Each girl thus perceives the rebuke differently—one as an act of rejection, one as a personal affront, one as a constructive comment. Consequently, each girl behaves differently in response to the same rebuke—one weeps, one becomes angry and one tries to do her job better.

It is important to notice that attitudes are persistent—they do not come and go but remain as a constant factor in our approach to our environment. They affect both the way we perceive situations and our behaviour in them. Many attempts have been made to define them; perhaps the two best known are those of Allport (1935) and Krech and Crutchfield (1948). The first states that: 'An attitude is a mental and neural state of readiness, organized through experience, exerting a directive or dynamic influence upon the individual's response to all objects and situations with which it is related.' The second says that: 'An attitude can be defined as an enduring organization of motivational, emotional, perceptual and cognitive processes with respect to some aspect of the individual's world.' Both definitions lay emphasis on the organization of attitudes into what amounts to an enduring 'frame of reference' through which the individual perceives his world, a frame which exerts a significant influence upon his behaviour and an understanding of which is therefore required if his behaviour is to be understood.

Attitudes are not motives, although they are closely linked with motives. A motive is any condition of the organism that affects its readiness to start a sequence of behaviour. It can arise from the physiological state of the organism (e.g. the hunger drive), from prior learning (e.g. the motive for success) or from momentary set (e.g. noticing an apple on a tray on the sideboard). Motives have goals, e.g. to reduce hunger, to achieve success, to enjoy the apple. Attitudes are concerned with objects, concepts or situations. A man may be motivated by his need for food (his goal—to eat) so that he adopts a daring attitude towards wild animals (objects). He may be motivated by his desire for success (his goal—to achieve recognition by his fellow men) so that he adopts a hard-working attitude towards life (situation).

There are two main differences between attitudes and motives:

(1) *Attitudes are more persistent than motives.* For example, a man will not be constantly motivated to eat but he may persistently maintain his daring attitude to wild animals so that he learns to enjoy hunting for 'sport'. Or a man will not be motivated to use every occasion to achieve recognition from others—he may like to retire occasionally to his study with

31

a book—but his hardworking attitude persists so that he may continue even with the most abstruse treatise to the end.

(2) *A motive is more specific than an attitude.* For example, a man with a daring attitude towards wild animals in general is, at a given moment, motivated to hunt and kill this particular one. A man with a hardworking attitude to life is, at a given moment, motivated to direct his energies towards the passing of some particular examination or to bring off some particular business deal. Attitudes are thus generally more persistent and more inclusive than motives.

Attitudes seem to be built up during our life experience in four different ways:

(1) *Through early environmental experience.* For example, from an investigation into authoritarian attitudes, Sanford (1959) concluded 'that the high-authoritarians come, for the most part, from homes in which a rather stern and distant father dominated a submissive and long-suffering but morally restrictive mother, and in which discipline was an attempt to apply conventionally approved rules rather than an effort to further general values in accordance with the perceived needs of the child.' The early environment seems to be an important factor in the formation of many attitudes which persist through the whole of a lifetime. Newcomb and Svehla (1937) report correlations between parents' and children's attitudes as follows: towards the church, 0·63; towards war, 0·44; towards communism, 0·56. They claim that parental consistencies or inconsistencies of attitude tend to be reflected in the children.

(2) *Through general experience.* The boy with a weakly body finds himself involved in a fight with another and stronger boy. He may fight back courageously enough at first but in

the end is beaten and knocked to the ground. Further similar experiences follow; on every occasion the boy is thrashed. In the end, he tries to avoid situations in which he may find himself threatened by other and stronger boys. So he builds up an evasive attitude towards situations in which physical violence seems likely and this attitude persists throughout his life. He may of course react to the situation in some other way, for example, by trying to flatter the bully so that he will not hit him. He adopts a fawning attitude towards those who possess power and might use it to hurt him; he becomes the court flatterer, the 'toady', the sycophant.

(3) *Through some traumatic experience.* A schoolboy whose family had offered lavish hospitality to a boy from a European capital city, taking him on visits to all the key places of interest in and around London, made a return visit to stay with the foreign boy and his parents. Instead of taking time to show the schoolboy the sights of their great city, the foreign family was busy all the time on its own devices. Even the boy neglected his English visitor to play tennis with his friends. The English boy returned home in a very bitter mood, having adopted a resentful attitude towards all Europeans, an attitude he still retains years later. One single experience can sometimes be so wounding as to shape an attitude which endures for a lifetime.

(4) *Through imitation.* A great many attitudes tend to be copied from those of parental or other authority or prestige figures. We have seen already that children tend to copy attitudes held by their parents. When young people in adolescence break away from the parental environment and its influence they are still often not strong enough to work out their own attitudes to situations and look instead for a hero figure or prestige group whose attitudes they may copy. It is not only adolescents and children however who look around

33

for a strong person to copy. Managers may hesitate to formulate their attitudes until they have discovered those held by the managing director and, if theirs tend to conflict, will sometimes reshape them to conform to his. When a new situation arises on the shop floor, men may wait to find out the attitude of the shop steward before deciding what their own will be. Most of us retain a hint of the insecure adolescent in our make-up when it comes to forming attitudes.

The groups to which we belong also exercise a strong influence upon us in our attitude formation. If someone is made vividly aware of his membership of some particular group, perhaps by being sent regularly quantities of approving literature about it, an effect described by Kelley (1955) as 'salience', there is considerable evidence that this has a significant effect in shaping his attitudes to those which the group will approve. Charters and Newcomb (1947) describe a study which suggests that 'an individual's expression of attitudes is a function of the relative momentary potency of his relevant group membership'. This would mean, for example, that the student who moves from university into a business house or industrial firm will tend to change his attitudes from those approved by his student friends to others which will gain the approval of members of his new significant group. So we see the long-haired student a year later as a smartly dressed young man about town. Similar changes in attitude are seen when men are promoted from the shop floor to management or when wild young women grow into mothers with teen-aged daughters.

Sometimes the group which shapes our attitudes is the larger one of our society as a whole. Here we find ourselves conforming to attitudes which belong to our particular culture. Western attitudes towards the role of women in society are today very different from those held a hundred years ago; they are very different too from those still held in many parts

34

of the East. Although women would scarcely claim that they have yet achieved full equality with men, it is no longer strange in the West to find women doctors, lawyers, scientists, teachers, journalists, bus conductors, personnel managers and politicians, for example. In many Eastern countries, women's role is still seen as essentially contained within the home and family. In more limited social groupings, Margaret Mead (1928 and 1930) discovered significant differences in cultural attitudes towards sex between Samoans and the Manus of New Guinea; Samoans took a liberal attitude towards sex, Manus a repressive one. Ruth Benedict (1934) has stressed the power of cultural attitudes in shaping human behaviour among the Zuñi of New Mexico, the Dobuans of New Guinea and the Kwakiutl of Vancouver Island.

It is important to recognize the extent to which changes in our attitudes bring about changes in our behaviour. Perhaps one of the best known examples of this is provided by the famous Hawthorne studies, recorded by Roethlisberger and Dickson (1943), an investigation into the behaviour of factory workers which began in 1927 at the Western Electric Company's Hawthorne Works at Chicago, USA. Some experiments had taken place on the effects on production by girl assembly workers of changes in the lighting in their departments. These involved two groups of girls, a control group and a test group. Groups were matched for numbers, experience and average production. The girls in the control group worked under a constant light strength; the girls in the test group worked under three different light intensities. Production rose in the test group, apparently because of the better lighting conditions. However, when the production of the control group was examined, it was found to have increased also and to about the same extent as for the test group. Whatever had caused the increase in production it had evidently not been the change in the lighting intensities. Various refinements of the experiment were then carried out, including the pretence that the light power had been increased when in fact it remained the same or had actually been lowered. Under each set of circumstances the new high level of production was maintained.

Following these first investigations, a more complex study was made over a period of five years. This involved six girls who were established as a team in a relay assembly test room. A complete daily record was kept of various changes that were made in the girls' working conditions—the introduction of rest pauses, free lunches, a shorter working week, higher rates of pay, less rigid supervision. The investigators wanted to see if they could correlate these variables with changes in production but found it impossible. They were perplexed by the general trend towards increased production independent of all these changes. At the end of their work, the investigators realized that the most important factor in the total situation was one they had themselves unwittingly introduced. The changes brought about by management in carrying out their investigation—the rest pauses, the free lunches, the shorter working week, the higher pay, the easier supervision—had combined to bring about a new social situation which had altered the girls' attitudes to their work and to each other. This new social situation, in creating this change in attitudes, had led to the increase in production.

If we want to understand human behaviour, we must look not only at the behaviour but at the human beings who behave. Not until we have gained some understanding of the attitudes which men and women hold towards the situations and social groupings with which they are involved can we begin to appreciate why they behave in them as they do. Hence the need for the interviewer to know something about attitudes, what they are, what they do, and how to discover them through his interviewing skills.

The interviewer must of course recognize that not only is the respondent's behaviour shaped by his attitudes; so is his own. This means that in any interview situation there are two sets of attitudes to be taken account of—the respondent's and the interviewer's. Either or both these sets may influence the interview so that the interviewer is prevented from seeing clearly and objectively the respondent and his problem and, as a consequence, the respondent cannot be helped to see clearly and objectively the problem situation in which he is involved. The interview thus ceases to be an effective act of communication; it becomes warped or biased. Bias is an important factor in any interview for, unless some way of controlling it can be found, the interview cannot achieve its objective. Our next task therefore is to look at the way in which bias can affect the interview and attempt to discover where bias lies and how it may either be eliminated or, at the least, have its effects minimized.

CHAPTER FOUR

The Effects of Bias

Bias has been defined by Drever (1952) as 'an attitude either for or against a particular theory, hypothesis or explanation, which unconsciously influences an individual's judgement.' In an interview situation, bias may appear (a) in the interviewer, (b) in the respondent, and (c) in the situation. For example, an interviewer may be biased for or against the respondent by his appearance, race, accent, age and many other factors. A respondent may be biased to answer in a certain way by the interviewer's clothes, accent, age, and so on. The situation itself may contain biasing factors; for example, a man may be biased to answer a clergyman's questions about how he feels towards the Church less honestly if he has come to see him to make arrangements for his daughter's wedding in church than if he has met him informally at a social gathering.

(a) One of the best known examples of *interviewer bias* is contained in an early investigation, reported by Rice (1929), to determine causes of destitution by interviewing men in flophouses and cheap hotels in America. Rice found that respondents interrogated by one interviewer (a temperance supporter) consistently assigned a high importance to drunkenness whereas the respondents of another interviewer (a social reformer) tended to emphasize social and industrial conditions. It seems that each interviewer 'heard' different things from similar groups of people. Guest (1947) used fifteen interviewers to interview *one* respondent. The interviews were recorded. Guest concluded from an analysis of the recorded interviews

38

that the interviewer's own attitudes helped to shape the interview because interviewers tended to introduce their own ideas into the conversation either by commenting on an answer made by the respondent or by suggesting appropriate answers when he appeared to be hesitant.

(b) *Respondent bias* is illustrated in a survey conducted by the National Opinion Research Centre and reported by Cantrill (1944). The survey took place in one of the southern states of America, using both white and coloured interviewers. It was found that negroes gave significantly different answers to white interviewers as against those they gave to interviewers of their own race. White interviewers obtained significantly higher proportions of conventionally acceptable answers than did negro interviewers Negroes seemed more reluctant to reveal to white interviewers their feelings over discrimination in employment, for example. In a classic study Katz (1942) showed that opinions reported by working-class interviewers were consistently more radical than those reported by middle-class interviewers who interviewed the same respondents. As all the interviewers used in the study had been carefully trained in interviewing techniques, Katz concluded that respondents tended to bias their responses to what they felt would be acceptable to the interviewer.

(c) Two key factors which seem to bring about *situational bias* are those of *anonymity* and *sponsorship*. Hyman (1954) reports evidence to show that respondents may give significantly different replies to questions depending on whether or not they think their responses will be able to be identified or on what organization they think is sponsoring the interviewer. The guarantee of anonymity does not of course assure more honest answering. Hyman points out that there is some indication that in Japan 'surveys where names were not taken might be answered in a more frivolous fashion because of the Japanese experience that any serious inquiry in the past involved the recording of names'. In occupied Germany after the war a survey was carried out by Crespi (1950), part of which was said to be sponsored by the American military government and part by a fictitious 'German opinion institute'. One third of the thirty-six questions yielded differences which were significant at the ·05 level, and five questions yielded differences significant at the ·01 level.

It may begin to appear that, as we all hold attitudes and are therefore liable to be biased in certain directions and as the people we are expected to interview are biased too and even the situations in which we will carry out the interview contain biasing factors, it is going to be extremely difficult to get at the truth in the interview. We cannot do a great deal to eliminate the respondent's bias though we may do something to help us recognize it but we can be careful about situational factors and we can do a great deal to check the effect of our own bias. The first thing needed is to accept the fact that we all are biased in some direction or other, perhaps about race or religion or politics, or colour or class or age or accent or appearance. Once we recognize that we have prejudices, we can begin to take account of them and attempt to eliminate their effects on our behaviour in the interview.

There seem to be two types of interviewer bias, (1) *ideological*, and (2) *expectational*. Ideological bias consists in evaluating the respondent's behaviour in terms of the ideology of the interviewer. This means in effect that the interviewer hears not what the respondent says but what he would like him to say. We have already mentioned the example of this reported by Rice (1929). Another study has been reported by Calahan, Tamulonis and Verner (1947) in which interviews taken by more than one hundred different interviewers were tabulated separately. About three quarters of the 51 interview questions showed significant differences in the responses obtained by different interviewers. Many of these differences were *in the direction* of the interviewers' own opinions. Apparently the interviewers tended to see respondents in their own image.

Further evidence has been provided by a study carried out by Cooper and Jahoda (1947). Subjects were asked to state what position was taken by a communicator on the prohibition question. It was found that there was a tendency for individuals whose position was close to that of the communicator to report the latter's position quite accurately, for individuals a little bit removed to report his position as substantially more like their own (termed 'assimilation effect') and for those with more discrepant positions to report the communicator's position as more extreme than it really was (termed 'contrast effect').

'These findings' would seem to suggest that interviewers tend to bias respondents' views into a position closely approximating their own only when they are not already very different. This may mean that ideological bias is not so serious a problem as some would suggest. Hyman (1954) has suggested that the interviewer's ideology is a lot less important in biasing responses than his simple expectation of what the responses are likely to be. To illustrate Hyman's point, let us imagine an interviewer who is extremely liberal in his attitudes to divorce and who is given the task of interviewing a clergyman. Hyman would say that he is not so likely to be biased to represent the clergyman's views as liberal like his own as he is to be biased by what he expects them to be. He may indeed report the clergyman's views as more rigid than they really are because this is what he expects.

Hyman resolves expectational bias into three types: (a) *attitude structure expectations*, (b) *role expectations*, and (c) *probability expectations*. The first two develop during the interview; the last one precedes it. An example of *attitude structure expectations* would be if, after two or three minutes of an interview, the interviewer were to say to himself: 'Ah, now I can see the way this person thinks; I know precisely what he'll say next.' And if he does not in fact say it, the interviewer still 'hears' him say it. This bias is based on the

41

belief that certain attitudes hang together so that, when the interviewer has heard two or three expressed, he expects the rest, he thinks he knows what they will be. He expects a certain consistency which he then reads into the interview even when it is not there. Smith and Hyman (1950) used a carefully recorded interview in which a respondent had been coached to take a strong internationalist position on foreign affairs but also, in answer to one particular question, to take an isolationist position. Only one fifth of the interviewers who listened to this recorded interview noted down the inconsistent isolationist response correctly. Their expectations, based on the respondent's replies to previous questions, apparently influenced their perception of an answer given later in the interview. An example of *role expectations* is when the interviewer, early on in an interview, says to himself, 'So this man is a shop steward; these shop stewards (or managers, or clergymen, or nurses, etc.) are all the same. I know the line he will take.' The respondent is seen as a member of a group rather than as an individual and all the attitudes normally associated with the group are consequently attributed to him. The interviewer may even ascribe attitudes to the respondent on the grounds of his appearance or dress or accent. He speaks with a Yorkshire accent therefore he is expected to be rough and tough in his attitudes, especially towards money. He is dressed in a peaked cap and overalls, therefore he is expected to take a favourable attitude towards trade unions. He wears a dark suit and bowler hat and carries a rolled umbrella so is expected to hold favourable attitudes to the Conservative party. An example of *probability expectations* is when the interviewer, before even the interview has started or he has met the respondent, says to himself, 'Of course he'll say he deserves more pay. Everybody thinks that.'

Expectation bias may not be kept by the interviewer to himself. It may also be articulated and this means that the respondent becomes aware of it and may respond by falling in with the interviewer's expectations or resisting them by lapsing into silence or perhaps an angry denial. An example of an *attitude structure expectation situation* arose when an interviewer, after hearing the first few responses, said with some enthusiasm, 'Ah good. It sounds to me as if you'd enjoy working with people.' The respondent, recognizing that this was approved, went out of his way to demonstrate how keen he was on working as a member of a team. The bias in the question thus led to a corresponding bias in the responses. An example of a *role expectation situation* was when an interviewer said rather hotly to a respondent, 'So you're a traffic warden. How many motorists have you managed to do down this morning?' The respondent gave him an angry look but continued with the interview though he confined himself as far as possible to monosyllabic grunts and gave as little information as he could to the interviewer. In a *probability expectation situation*, a hurried interviewer said at the beginning of the interview, 'Well, I'm sure you'd agree with most people that there is something radically wrong with the youth of today,' to which the respondent replied, 'I would not agree any such thing.' The interviewer, somewhat taken aback, then said, 'Well, perhaps you'd tell me what you do think about the youth of today.' The respondent thereupon entered into a long defence of young people which may have been biased in favour of young people to a degree not normally held by him. Afterwards he said, 'People are always criticizing the youngsters. I suspect they're all a bit jealous. I felt I had to lay into him a bit.'

Spoken ideological comments can also upset the balance of an interview and introduce bias on the part of the respondent. A company employee, being interviewed for a supervisory post, made the remark, 'I'm inclined to feel the piece work system we use here has a great many weaknesses.' The interviewer, a manager, commented enthusiastically, 'I must say I agree with you about that.' Such evaluative statements bias the respondent to say the sort of thing he realizes will be approved of, especially if he is particularly anxious to impress the interviewer—as in this instance where the manager had considerable influence in the making of the appointment. If the interviewer had confined himself to making an encouraging remark to draw the respondent out, for example, 'That is interesting. Tell me a bit more about your ideas on this,' he would have helped the respondent to develop his point and have learned something more about the way he really saw the pay situation in the company. Kahn and Cannell (1957) have written: 'The interview consistently rewards full and complete response, rewards responses focused on the objectives of the interview, and tends to discourage communications irrelevant to those objectives. Interviewer bias occurs when the rewarding and discouraging activities of the interviewer are not limited to these areas.' Hildum and Brown (1956) describe a telephone questionnaire administered to male college students on general education. The questionnaire contained fifteen statements, some expressing a favourable attitude to general education, some an unfavourable. Subjects had to choose between four responses: Agree strongly, agree slightly, disagree slightly, and disagree strongly. Some of the students were reinforced for each response indicating a favourable attitude by the use of the word 'Good' and some were reinforced for unfavourable attitudes. The responses were found to be biased significantly in the direction of verbal reinforcement. It seems likely then that evaluative remarks and gestures like frowns, a pleased expression, movements of the head that would seem to indicate approval or disapproval, should be avoided in case the interviewer unintentionally betray his own attitude and so bias the respondent.

It is important then that interviewers recognize their biases and take account of them when conducting the interview. This is true for all interviews, not least for those with people who are disturbed by some problem situation. To be able to see other people as they really are, that is, without being influenced by our biases, demands that we know a good deal about ourselves. We cannot learn to accept others until we have first learned to accept ourselves, and we cannot help others until we are able to accept them as they are and for what they are. The interview is a conversation; the last thing it must be allowed to become is an argument, for this means it ceases to be an interview. Yet there is the danger that this can happen if the interviewer is unaware of, and therefore unable to take account of, his biases. *Rapport* can be quickly broken down and the interview come to an untimely end.

CHAPTER FIVE

Carrying out the Interview

I. ESTABLISHING RAPPORT

In formal selection or appraisal type interviews it is of course possible to prepare for the interview by fixing a time, arranging a room with comfortable chairs and a table, having paper and pen available and examining application forms, reports and notes before the interview takes place. Sometimes this is possible also with a problem-solving interview: an employee with a problem may ask for the opportunity to discuss his difficulty in his employer's office and at an arranged time. But many such interviews inevitably take place without any kind of preliminary arrangement: a worried patient bursts out with his problem to a nurse in a ward; an angry employee comes unexpectedly into the supervisor's office with a grievance about the rate for the job; an anxious parishioner takes the opportunity provided by the clergyman's visit to reveal some family distress; a parent may waylay her child's schoolteacher in the street. Sometimes it may be possible to delay the interview and arrange an easier time and more convenient place but sometimes the matter has to be dealt with there and then. If so, the interviewer must not allow himself to become flustered or embarrassed. It is important to be patient, understanding, calm and, above all, to be seen to be willing to listen. Let the person with the problem get the first emotional surge out of his system. After that, he may be able to approach his problem more rationally and the very fact that somebody has shown himself willing to listen may not only enable him to deal more constructively with it but give him confidence that the listener is ready to support him as he attempts to deal with it.

This confident and permissive relationship between interviewer and respondent is one of *rapport*; the respondent is able to feel that the interviewer is genuinely interested in him as a person and will listen willingly to all he wants to tell him. *Rapport* does not mean 'chumminess'; a certain social distance is appropriate to the role relationship between interviewer and respondent. The danger with over-friendliness is that the respondent may become biased to say what he feels is pleasing to the interviewer and to avoid telling him of incidents which might place him in an unfavourable light. To please his interviewer he may even agree at the end of the interview that he now knows how to deal with his problem when in fact he is as confused about it as ever. *Rapport* is equally important for both the formal and informal interview. In the more formal interview, the interviewer can ensure that he will not be interrupted by telephone calls or messages. This is a matter of simple common sense. A respondent who has taken ten or fifteen minutes to settle down and is just about to talk openly and frankly about his problem may have to break off to allow his interviewer to take a phone call. At the end of the call, the respondent may find it very difficult to return to the mood of the moment before the telephone rang. He may feel it incongruous that the interviewer could turn his attention away from what seems to him his all-demanding problem and so become unable to continue the interview effectively. The net consequence is that the telephone call not merely interrupted the interview, it terminated it with the consequent loss of a valuable part of the interviewer's time and a breakdown in confidence in the interviewer by the respondent, a breakdown which cannot be easily mended.

II. BEGINNING THE INTERVIEW

If the interview has been arranged beforehand, the interviewer should greet the respondent courteously on his arrival and, if necessary, introduce himself. Imagine that an employee, Mr Brown, has asked for a confidential interview about a personal problem with his personnel manager, Mr Jones. Here are three alternative ways it might begin:

(a) *Mr Jones* (standing up): Good morning, Mr Brown. Do come and sit down. Would you like a cigarette?
Mr Brown: Thank you.
Mr Jones: Light?
Mr Brown: Thank you.
Mr Jones: It has turned out very cold this morning. Makes one realize winter is on the way.
Mr Brown: Yes. It won't be long now. Still, we had a good summer.
Mr Jones: We certainly can't complain. Well now, I understand you'd like to have a chat with me about a personal matter.

(b) *Mr Jones* (seated): Ah, you're Mr Brown are you? Sit down. What do you want to see me about?

(c) *Mr Jones* (seated): Come in. Ah yes—now you're ... (looks through papers on his desk) ... sorry, I just can't place you. What's your name?
Mr Brown: Brown, sir. I asked for an appointment.
Mr Jones: Oh yes. Well, sit down. I'd better warn you I'm in rather a hurry. I've got an important meeting in ten minutes, so you'd better get on with it.

It is scarcely necessary to comment on which opening is most likely to prove effective in establishing *rapport*.

At the beginning of the interview it is important to *clarify its objective.* In interview (*a*), Mr Jones raises the question of why Mr Brown wants to see him so that Mr Brown may follow this up by setting his purpose for requesting the interview in fairly specific terms. The conversation might then continue like this:

Mr Brown: That's right, Mr Jones. I asked my foreman to arrange for me to see you.
Mr Jones: Good. Well, can you tell me what it's all about?
Mr Brown: Yes sir, of course. Well, it's about my lad ... he is eighteen now. He has always been a bit of a handful; not a bad boy really but troublesome.
Mr Jones: There are plenty of boys like that.
Mr Brown: I know. That is what the wife and I have always said; 'We're not the only ones.'
Mr Jones: Has he been playing you up?
Mr Brown: I'm afraid so. He's been coming in at all hours recently. And never telling us where he's been or who he's been with. It's been a real worry to us both.
Mr Jones: Mm hmm.
Mr Brown: When we'd ask, he'd tell us to mind our own business. He never used to cheek us up like that. But once or twice recently he's threatened to leave home. He could too; he's earning good money labouring on a building site. Not that I ever wanted him in a dead end job like that; I'd have liked him to do an apprenticeship but he wasn't interested. Said there wasn't enough money in it for him. Anyway I've never said too much. I felt I mustn't drive him away from home or I'd lose the little bit of influence I did have with him.
Mr Jones: Yes, I can see that.
Mr Brown: Well, one of my mates was walking home with me the other night and he opened up and told me he'd seen Harry driving round in big cars with two or three real bad

'uns. The sort who had been in trouble with the law. I can tell you I'm really worried about it.
Mr Jones: You feel Harry may be heading for real trouble.
Mr Brown: I'm afraid so. I didn't tell the wife but it's been on my mind since I heard. I just don't know what to do for the best—whether to tackle Harry and stand the chance of a first-class row and maybe have him leave home or just say nothing. I've got to talk it through with somebody?

Mr Jones leads Mr Brown to the point where he can define the purpose of the interview precisely—to talk through the problem of his worry about his son with a view to seeing if it will help him decide what action to take.

It is clear that when the initiative for the interview lies with the respondent, as in the example above, the clarification of the purpose of the interview will not be possible until the interview has progressed some way. The interviewer's first objective must be to obtain this; only then can he go on to conduct an effective interview. So many interviews take place in which this is not done with the result that interviewer and respondent get at cross purposes with each other. The interviewer, because he has not defined his objectives, asks questions or steers the interview to areas that seem inappropriate to the respondent. He in turn becomes irritated, feels that the interviewer is pushing him where he does not want to go, and leaves the interview feeling that the whole thing was largely a waste of time.

In some situations of course the interviewer will not have sent for the respondent and must himself begin by explaining the purpose of the interview. After the initial preliminaries, the interviewer might say, for example: 'I understand from your supervisor that you feel you have been overlooked in one or two promotion possibilities recently and that you have been upset by this. Can you tell me about it?' The purpose of the interview is thus clarified—to discuss the respondent's disappointment when, as he sees it, he has been overlooked for promotion. The respondent now knows precisely what his conversation with the interviewer is to be about (its specific context) and that its purpose is to discuss his feelings to this. Whoever initiates the interview, and it may be either the interviewer or the respondent, it is still the interviewer's responsibility to clarify its purpose. Only when a purpose has been stated which is accepted as valid by both interviewer and respondent can an effective interview take place. The respondent must see the purpose of the interview as supporting his own goals, otherwise his interaction with the interviewer—if it takes place at all—will not be directed to helping the interview move forward in a positive manner.

III. LOOKING FOR BEHAVIOURAL EVIDENCE

During the interview the respondent will express some of his likes and dislikes, i.e. his attitudes to various objects, concepts or situations. He may say, for example, that he is keen on reading. The interviewer may simply note this, in which case he has received a rather vague bit of information and no proof that it is true other than the respondent's unverified claim. The interviewer may however want to check on the statement with a view to discovering rather more detailed information with which the respondent may back up his claim. So he asks him what kind of books he enjoys most. The respondent may reply that he enjoys historical books. Again the interviewer may simply note the fact, in which case he has once again obtained a somewhat vague bit of information, though a little more precise than the first bit, or he may check on the statement still further. 'That is interesting,' he may say. 'What period of history do you most like reading about?' If the respondent says that he is particularly interested in the history of the Russian Revolution, he can be asked what book on the subject he has enjoyed most or has read most recently. If he replies that he has recently read Isaac Deutscher's biography of Stalin, the interviewer, whether he has himself read the book or not, can ask what he thought about it and why. The respondent's capacity to provide a coherent answer at each step of this questioning process provides a validation of his original claim to enjoy reading.

I heard a young manager ask a school leaver if she got on well with other girls. She replied 'Oh yes,' to which he responded by saying 'Jolly good.' His only evidence for the truth of her claim was however her own unvalidated statement. He might have got some real evidence by questioning her about her past behaviour in situations in which she had been in contact with other girls. At school had she ever been a form captain or prefect? Did she spend her leisure time alone or with a group of friends? What sort of things had she done in company with others? (there is a difference between tagging along on a school outing and helping to organize a camping expedition to Iceland). Had she ever been in a position in which other people had accepted her as an authority figure—in Guides? Youth group? School club or committee? Answers to these questions would have given him some behavioural evidence on which to base his judgement as to whether or not the girl would be likely to get on with other girls in the future.

People's claims about themselves always need to be checked against behavioural evidence. Someone says, 'I'm interested in foreign travel.' We can best discover what this means by trying to find out how the respondent has expressed this interest in his past behaviour. If he can claim simply to have read a good many books about foreign travel, that is one thing; if he can claim to have travelled extensively throughout Europe and the Middle East, that is quite another.

In a selection interview, I heard a young girl asked, 'How long have you been in your present job?' She replied without hesitation, 'Seven years.' The interviewer at once interpreted this as meaning she had been in her present company for seven years and later claimed that she was a 'sticker' and not the sort of girl who moved around a lot. 'Give her the job and she will stay,' he asserted. A second interviewer, however, had taken the precaution of checking her statement. 'So you have been with the A.B.C. company seven years?' he asked. 'Oh no,' she replied, 'only three. I was with the R.S.T. company for two years before that and I also worked for a small export office for a couple of years. I meant I had been a shorthand typist for seven years. But only the last three with A.B.C.' This gave quite a different picture of the girl's attitudes to moving around.

Probing for behavioural evidence is a guard against making unwarranted assumptions. 'We have a policy of no racial discrimination,' says a personnel officer. 'We simply appoint the best man to the job, irrespective of race or colour.' This can so easily be assumed to mean that the company carries out its declared policy and that no racial discrimination is to be found there. But when the interviewer goes on to ask how many coloured supervisors are at work in the company, how many coloured workers have been included in supervisory training schemes, how many coloured school-leavers have been awarded apprenticeships and finds that in each case the answer is none, he may begin to question his first assumption that the company carries out its policy of non-discrimination. Equally, if the company can in fact provide numbers of those who do hold such jobs or engage in such training, he may feel with some justification that the company is trying to implement its policy.

The danger of jumping to conclusions about what people mean when they make statements concerning their attitudes is always with us. In many cases, of course, people simply do not know what their attitudes are for these may operate below the level of consciousness. To say to someone, 'We like people who are flexible. Are you flexible?' is not only a leading question in that it points the respondent to the 'right' answer;

it may also be an impossible question for the respondent simply may not know himself well enough to be able to answer it. The interviewer, if he is to obtain a valid answer to the question, must search for instances of past behaviour in the respondent's life where he has displayed behaviour patterns that can be characterized as 'flexible' or 'inflexible'. This may not be so easy as asking the question directly but if any such patterns can be discovered the interviewer is able to obtain valid information. The respondent's own answer to the direct question is likely to be almost valueless for if he has little self-understanding it is uninformed and, if he has some degree of self-understanding, he may be biased to conceal the truth from the interviewer. There is also the sheer difficulty of communication by the use of words to be taken into account (we shall look at this in section IX) which on its own may lead to misunderstanding for the interviewer and respondent may not mean precisely the same thing by the word 'flexible'. To look carefully and systematically at the respondent's behaviour is the only way of obtaining evidence from which the interviewer can make a valid assessment of his attitudes.

IV. THE USE OF GENERAL QUESTIONS

General questions may best be understood as open-ended questions which enable the respondent to answer in his own words and to whatever extent he wishes to develop his answer. Specific questions lead usually to yes/no type answers. 'Do you like historical books?' is a specific question which leads to the response 'yes' or 'no'. 'What kind of books do you enjoy most?' is a general question which enables the respondent to describe what books he enjoys; it does not tie his answer to his attitude towards a specific group of books, in this case, historical books.

Once I heard an interviewer ask: 'Did you do particularly well during your schooldays?' The respondent answered, 'Oh yes.' The interviewer continued, 'They were happy days, were they?' Again the respondent answered, 'Yes.' The interviewer then passed on to another topic. If he had asked the general question, 'How do you feel about your time at school?' the respondent would have been given the chance to say something more explicit about her attitudes. The trouble with specific questions is that they tend to tie the conversation to what is in the interviewer's mind when the purpose of the interview is to enable the respondent to state and discuss what is in his mind. In the example quoted above, the theme of schooldays was related to doing 'particularly well' and to being 'happy'. As came out in a subsequent interview, the real importance of the respondent's schooldays lay in neither of these areas but in learning, with the help of a sympathetic teacher, not to be discouraged by a first failure but to work hard for a second attempt. The acceptance of her own limitations and the determination to set realistic but challenging objectives for herself seemed among her most important characteristics and these went back to her early experiences of failure and success at school. The interviewer's questions on doing 'particularly well' and being 'happy' gave no opportunity for these to be discovered or discussed. A series of general questions in a subsequent interview however gave the respondent the opportunity to reveal the real value of her schooldays. Part of the interview went like this:

(A) How do you feel about your time at school?
(B) Well, school taught me a lot, I suppose. I don't mean just academically but ... you know ... about life.
(A) What sort of things?
(B) I think probably most of all about myself ... as a person ... I wasn't specially good at lessons but I used to pass my exams each time. Then once I came an awful cropper. I hadn't really worked, I suppose, but I'd still expected to pass. I felt deflated. I'd never gone down like this before. My parents were

not much help, I remember. But Miss Henderson—she was one of my teachers—made me face up to myself and told me I'd simply got to do it all over again and pass this time. And I did. I lost a year over it though. Well, I didn't lose it exactly for I learned so many things from the experience.

(A) Can you tell me what sort of things?

(B) Well, I think I learned to accept disappointment without being defeated by it. I think I've come to believe about myself that I can do things in the end even if I can't do them the first time. Mind you, there are lots of things I can't do, I know that. But there are things I can do—if I try hard enough. I think that was probably the most important thing about my schooldays.

Because specific questions tend to reflect what is in the interviewer's mind, they also often become what are termed *leading questions*. A leading question is one in which the interviewer 'leads' the respondent towards making the 'right' reply, that is, the response acceptable to, or expected by, the interviewer. The questions 'Did you do particularly well during your schooldays?' and 'They were happy days, were they?' almost suggest that 'yes' is the required response and certainly the respondent gave this answer on each occasion although, as we saw from the second interview with her, this was not strictly true.

Take the question which I once heard a manager put to a young man who had applied for a job with his company: 'In this organization we require young men who are determined to get on. Now are you determined to get on?' There was clearly only one 'right' answer if the young man wanted the job and he duly gave it. In an interview with a young girl the interviewer asked, 'You're quite accustomed to handling the mail?' She replied, 'Yes.' He went on, 'This would be confidential mail. You would know not to discuss its contents with anybody?' He had made it quite clear that he wanted the answer 'yes' and once again he received it. He might well report eventually that the job applicant was accustomed to handling confidential mail and was very much aware of the need for secrecy regarding its contents but he had in fact gained no real evidence that these statements were true.

General questions enable a conversation to flow because they give the respondent the opportunity to say all that he wants to about the topic under discussion and do not tie him to particular or specific aspects of it. Of course specific questions have their own use—normally the gathering of factual information, e.g. 'Which department do you work in?' 'What school did you attend?' 'Did you get any "A" levels?' and so on. They are also useful in checking information offered, e.g. 'So your next step is to see the chairman?' 'Do I understand that you have already put in your application for this job?' 'I think you said that you had left school at sixteen?' 'It says here that your last job was with Smith & Jones. Is that correct?' These are all valuable questions and they help in sorting out facts but for the discovery of attitudes general questions are essential.

V. 'REFLECTING' FEELINGS

One of the most important skills needed in the problem-solving interviews is that of 'reflecting' feelings. This is a selective form of listening in which the interviewer picks out the emotional overtones of a statement and 'reflects' these back to the respondent without making any attempt to evaluate them. This means that the interviewer expresses neither approval nor disapproval, neither sympathy nor condemnation. Because the respondent may be in an emotional state, sympathy is liable to make him want to lean on the interviewer for support while criticism is liable to make him feel resentful and angry. Any attempt to get the respondent to look objectively and rationally at his problem at this stage is also likely to fail;

he is still too confused and upset to be able to do this and will intepret the very attempt as criticism.

Take the example of an employee who bursts out with the emotional statement: 'I've given up looking for promotion in this firm. Everybody is against me.' If the interviewer were sympathetically to say, 'You certainly seem to have had a raw deal,' he is simply paving the way for a probably lengthy, exaggerated and self-pitying account of all the firm's misdemeanours. The respondent will clutch at the opportunity of gaining sympathy rather than seek to deal positively with his problem. If however the interviewer sounds critical by saying, 'Oh stop being sorry for yourself,' the respondent is likely to react angrily, believing that here is yet another person who fails to understand him. An attempt to handle the problem on a purely rational level by saying, 'Of course they aren't. You're just imagining it,' will equally be rejected as a failure on the part of the interviewer to understand. He is convinced that what he is saying is true; to be told that he is 'imagining' it is to be made to feel foolish. His reaction to the interviewer is liable to be an angry one.

A 'reflection' of the respondent's statement means simply that the interviewer takes it and expresses it back to the respondent but in his own words, for example, 'You feel you haven't had a fair chance.' This statement offers neither sympathy nor criticism, nor is it made on a purely rational level; it is simply a statement of how the interviewer perceives the respondent's feelings. There is an implication of understanding: 'I understand what you are saying; I understand how you feel.' The interviewer makes no evaluation; he simply accepts the respondent's feelings about the situation and shows that he understands. This permissive behaviour enables the respondent to open up and begin to express his feelings at greater length. When grievances, frustrations, difficulties, problem situations of any sort are able to be expressed, the emotional overtones become clear and the respondent is then able to look at them more rationally and objectively. This gives the interviewer the opportunity, by appropriate questioning, to lead the respondent on to make constructive suggestions about his own situation.

Maier (1955) has suggested ten points to be observed in using the 'reflecting' technique:

(1) The interviewer should reflect the respondent's feelings in his own words rather than serve as a mimic or parrot;

(2) Remarks should be prefaced by 'You feel . . .', 'You think . . .', 'It seems to you that . . .'. Later in the interview these prefaces may be dropped.

(3) Reflected remarks should be formulated as statements and not as questions;

(4) It is important to wait out pauses. The respondent may be trying to sort out his thoughts and may be on the verge of expressing them when the interviewer breaks in with a question or remark;

(5) When many feelings are expressed, only the last one should be reflected;

(6) Only feelings actually expressed should be reflected. It is dangerous for the interviewer to start guessing at feelings which he thinks may be there;

(7) When inconsistent feelings are expressed, the interviewer should proceed as if no inconsistency had taken place;

(8) If a person cries during an interview, the interviewer may make reference to the fact so long as the respondent is not attempting to hide the tears;

(9) Decisions, solutions and constructive ideas may be reflected when these predominate over feelings of confusion, hostility, fear, insecurity, rejection, and the like;

(10) In reflecting another's state of mind, any indication of approval or disapproval is to be avoided.

We include below a number of statements which might be made in interviews by a respondent. The reader is asked to decide which of the alternative interviewer responses is an appropriate reflection and then to check it against the list of correct reflections given on page 61.

I. *No, I didn't get on awfully well in the Army.*
a. That was rather bad luck, wasn't it?
b. Oh, I think you did quite well; after all you got a commission.
c. It seems the Army was really too tough for you.
d. You feel you might have done better.

II. *I suppose I've always had a bit of an inferiority complex; it began when I was a child, I think. My mother used to say, 'Keep quiet; what do you know about it?' I still don't like to venture my opinions.*
a. Aren't you putting too much blame on your mother?
b. You feel hesitant about expressing your views.
c. Your mother seems to have been rather overbearing.
d. I find you quite intelligent.

III. *I prefer to work on my own initiative.*
a. You like to organize things your own way.
b. You are a solitary sort of person then?
c. In our company we work as a team.
d. You feel you don't get along well with other people.

IV. *I went to that church every Sunday for months and nobody ever spoke to me once.*
a. I quite understand how you feel.
b. It doesn't say much for the Vicar, does it?
c. That is just typical of too many churches these days.
d. You feel nobody was interested.

V. *I tried everything I could to make a go of things. But nothing I could do was ever right with her. It was nag, nag,*

nag from morning till night. In the end she packed up her things, took the child and went off to her mother. Of course everybody blames me. She can tell the tale so well, everyone thinks she is perfect and the fault is all on my side.
a. You mustn't lose heart so easily.
b. Don't you think it's important not to lose touch with the child?
c. You feel people are putting all the blame on you.
d. I should say you were both at fault.

VI. *Everyone is against you when you're young—parents, schoolteachers, police, the newspapers, the lot. Anything goes wrong and it's always your fault, never theirs. You get so fed up sometimes you'd just like to walk out on the lot of them.*
a. You feel pretty badly treated.
b. I don't think things are quite as black as you've painted them.
c. Don't run away from your problems.
d. You just want to get away from everyone.

VII. *I've given up praying. It doesn't seem to make any difference at all. When my wife was so ill, I prayed every day. She died just the same. And in such pain. I can't believe in prayer after that. It seems no use any more.*
a. You felt your prayers were not answered.
b. Perhaps your prayers were answered in another way.
c. I do understand how you feel about your wife's death.
d. You feel you can't see any point in prayer any more.

Correct reflections are as follows: I, *d*; II, *b*; III, *a*; IV, *d*; V, *c*; VI, *d*; VII, *d*.

'Reflecting' feelings is a skill which demands considerable practice. If it is done effectively, it gives the respondent a great deal of confidence in the capacity of the interviewer to understand him; as a result he is encouraged to talk openly about the problems that lie at the root of his worry. To reflect inaccurately however is to head for disaster. The inaccurate reflection is perceived by the respondent as yet another failure on the part of society to understand him. The respondent tends to disagree, argue or become silent and the interview consequently to break down.

'I always seem to have the worst possible luck,' says the respondent. 'The very day after I had accepted a job with another company and before I'd told my boss, my own company offered me promotion to a job I'd always had my eye on and I just could not take it because I was too deeply committed with the new company. I remember when I was a young man I went abroad and, a week after I had gone, the girl I was in love with broke off her engagement to another man. If I'd been around I might have been in the running but I didn't even know about it till I returned to England three years later and found her married to somebody else. It always seems to be like that with me.' The experienced interviewer reflects, 'You feel life really has got it in for you,' and the respondent answers, 'Yes, I do. That's it exactly,' and proceeds with his story, convinced that here is someone who understands him. The less competent interviewer makes a poor reflection, 'You feel you just cannot cope with life.' This is not what the respondent said and he is likely to see it as critical and to respond angrily with some such remark as, 'I never said that,' or even begin to argue that he has coped pretty well with a life that has been so unfair to him.

When an interviewer reflects and the respondent replies by saying, 'That's it exactly. That is just how I feel,' or 'Yes, indeed, that is just it,' the interviewer may be fairly sure that he has reflected accurately. But it takes time, practice and a good deal of experience in real life situations before an interviewer will feel confident that he can reflect accurately on most occasions.

VI. PROBING—LOOKING FOR SIGNIFICANT REMARKS

The search for behavioural evidence essentially involves probing, picking up significant areas for investigation and asking appropriate questions to draw relevant information from the respondent. The interviewer must be on the look-out all the time for the remark, the aside comment, that looks as if it might be worth further investigation. In an interview the respondent made the comment, 'Of course I'll never get promotion now; I'm a bit too old for that.' The interviewer let the remark go unquestioned and passed on to another topic. But how did the respondent feel about promotion prospects? Was his belief that he was too old for promotion sincerely held? Did this belief about his job prospects affect his attitudes to life and work? What were his feelings about himself and his abilities? These were all important questions if the respondent was to be understood as a person but the interviewer bypassed them completely. A district nurse in an interview commented on her job: 'I like it; there is more freedom than being in a hospital. You're working on your own but you're working with people too.' Here was a remark which, if followed up by careful probing, might have given a considerable amount of information about the nurse's attitudes to authority, responsibility and other people. Unfortunately the interviewer missed the opportunity to discover any of these through failure to probe what the nurse meant by her statement.

This failure to pick up significant remarks and to probe for the attitudes that lie behind them is a key factor in making the interview ineffective. Guest (1947), in an analysis of fifteen interviews, reported that the most frequent errors were all in the area of inadequate probing and recording of free responses. In an investigation reported by Hyman (1954) involving sixty-one interviewers on the National Opinion Research Council's permanent field staff, inadequate probing was again noted as

63

a major error. Four experienced members of N.O.R.C's professional staff claimed that in forty per cent of the instances where the interviewers should have probed they failed to do so. Not only that but, of the probes they suggested for the remaining sixty per cent, the expert judges decided that one fifth were inadequate. This meant that error in probing occurred in fifty-two per cent of the instances where probing was considered by the experts as necessary; forty per cent due to a failure to probe at all and another twelve per cent due to a failure to probe adequately.

Skill in probing demands complete attention to all that the respondent says and the way he says it. The interviewer may need the sensitivity to recognize not only the significant remark but the significant omission, the remark the respondent did not make which one might reasonably have expected him to do. The respondent who, in discussing perhaps the problems involved in changing his job from London to Belfast, makes no reference to his ever having discussed them with his wife, may in fact be 'saying' something more significant by his omission than if he had stated that he and his wife had quarrelled violently over the projected move. It was Sherlock Holmes's realization that the dog did not bark during the night, when one might reasonably have expected it do so, that enabled him to solve the mystery of the disappearance of the race-horse Silver Blaze. It may be the interviewer's recognition of the significant omission that enables him to go on to ask the appropriate questions which will help to clarify the situation.

In probing, it is important for the interviewer to be sensitive to the need for silence. There is a world of difference between the embarrassing silence when interviewer or respondent may simply not know what to say next and the pregnant silence when the respondent is searching for the right words to express his feelings. His brow is furrowed, he looks away from the interviewer, his expression is thoughtful. For the interviewer to interpose another question at this point may well mean a failure to catch something important. I heard an interviewer ask a young man, 'What do you feel you really want from your job?' The young man hesitated. 'I'm not sure. I'm afraid I can probably only answer that question in negative terms. I don't just want money.' He stayed silent for a few moments, looking thoughtful, and the interviewer wisely held his tongue. The respondent spoke again, 'I think what I want most of all is to feel I'm doing something worth while.' The words came out fairly hurriedly as though he had just discovered something new about himself.

The skilled interviewer is all the time examining what the respondent says and asking himself 'Why?'—'Why did he say this?', 'Why did he behave like that?', 'Why did she change her school when she was fourteen?', 'Why did he leave his last job when he claims he was on the way to promotion?', 'Why does she want to be a secretary when she is half-way through her training as a nurse?', and so on.

Men and women who approach another human being with some 'complaint' or 'grievance' may not at first express the real problem that is at the root of their distress. This may be exposed only when the respondent has gained sufficient confidence in the interviewer. In some instances however the respondent may not be aware of what his real problem is and it may be only as a skilled interviewer helps him to examine his situation that he begins to understand what lies at the source of his worry. The interviewer probes not so that he may tell the respondent what precisely his problem is but primarily to enable the respondent to discover it for himself and to feel that, in doing so, he is able to share it with another person who understands him. The interviewer who rushes in, however accurately, to say, 'This is your problem' will be likely to meet resistance; the interviewer who waits until the respondent is able to say, 'I think I begin to see what my problem really is' will find that the respondent can not only now accept his problem as one of the facts of his life but that the interviewer is someone with whom he can share it. Resistance is replaced by acceptance. This approach removes from probing the stigma that it is unwarranted interference. The interviewer probes for the sake of the respondent and so that the respondent may begin to diagnose his problem, an essential preliminary to his coming to terms with it.

Below is given an example of a probing interview in which the respondent begins by stating that his problem is one thing and ends by recognizing that it is quite another. It takes place between the works manager of an engineering company, Mr Stewart, and a work study officer, Mr Knox.

K. I wondered if I could have a talk with you about my career prospects, Mr Stewart.

S. Of course. What's the problem?

K. Well, it's just that I've been in the work study department for a long time, seven years in fact, and I felt that maybe the time had come to make a move. I did apply for one or two jobs within the company—I even had an interview for one of them—but nobody seems to have considered me very seriously for them.

S. What jobs were they, Mr Knox?

K. The one I had the interview for was as supervisor of the test room. I think I'd have quite liked that. They gave the job to Mr Reid in the end. Of course he is younger than I am. That is partly what is so worrying. I feel I'm getting to the stage when I've got to make a move soon if I'm to make one at all.

S. Mm hmm.

K. I'm thirty-nine. It won't be long till I'm forty and you know how hard it is to change after that age. If I don't get promotion within the next couple of years, it may be too late. I'll really be in a rut.

S. I see.

K. Not that I would call the work study department a rut exactly; far from it. It's interesting and I enjoy my work. I'm never stuck in one place; I'm all over the factory. I never know from one day to the next what problems I'll be having to try to sort out.

S. Yes, I can understand that.

K. The work study department is all right. It's just that I feel I ought to have promotion. And it's now or never really.

S. You feel you have got to have promotion soon.

K. Yes. That's the way it seems to me.

S. What experience did you have before you went into work study?

K. Well, I did an engineering apprenticeship with the R.S.T. company, then I worked in the tool room at Armstrong's for five years and then I got a job in this company as a charge hand in the machine shop. That was before you came here, Mr Stewart. Actually, I didn't enjoy it much. It was repetitive production work. I was there for six years and, during the latter part of that time, I went to the local technical college and took a diploma course in work study. I did it off my own bat. I paid for it out of my own pocket too, but when I'd finished it the company reimbursed me and moved me into a better job in work study; they said I'd shown initiative. I've been doing it ever since; seven years it is now.

S. How about the money side of things?

K. Well, I've done all right in a way. I mean I've had regular increases. I suppose I shouldn't complain. But I could do with a bit more money. I've two children, a girl of ten and a boy of eight, and they're getting pretty expensive to keep. They've got to have all the same things as the neighbours' children; the wife insists on that. It's a bit of a thing with her. She is always buying them clothes. A better job would certainly help so far as money is concerned.

S. So really you feel you'd like promotion to something different partly because you want a change and partly because you'd like more money.

K. That's the situation in a nutshell, Mr Stewart.

S. On the other hand, you've said you enjoy your job in work study.

K. Oh indeed. I like it a lot. I'd be very sorry to leave it. It's always fascinated me. It's certainly not boring. It's the best job I've ever done.

S. Mm hmm.

K. To tell you the truth, if I could get some sort of promotion in work study, I'd be very happy. And I think it would satisfy the wife too.

S. Your wife would like to see you get promotion?

K. Well yes—it's only natural isn't it? You know how the womenfolk don't like their friends' husbands to outshine their own.

S. How do you mean?

K. Well, one chap gets made up to supervisory grade and all the other wives think their husbands should get made up too. It's a sort of game with them, I think. But it's hard luck on the poor husbands sometimes.

S. In what way?

K. Well, when you're doing a job you like you don't necessarily want to go changing it. All you want is a bit more money maybe. Women are born snobs, it seems to me. They're always at you to get on in life so they can bask in what they think is the reflected glory. But still, that's not what I came to talk about.

S. Mm hmm.

K. No, I came to talk about . . . well, about prospects in the company. As I said, I feel it's time I made a change.

S. You're anxious to get out of work study then?

K. Well, to be honest, Mr Stewart, no I'm not. What I'd really like is to get some kind of promotion within the

work study department, something that would give me a
bit more money and maybe a bit more responsibility.

S. You feel your wife would be happy with this too?

K. Oh, I think so. I think it would solve her problem completely.

Mr Stewart explores the problem with Mr Knox and sum-
marizes his desire for promotion as seeming to arise from the
fact that he wants a change and because he would like more
money so that his wife can keep the family up to the standards
imposed by their neighbours. Mr Knox admits his liking for
his job in the work study department and makes the remark
that even some kind of promotion in this department 'would
satisfy the wife'. Mr Stewart at once picks up this second
significant reference to Mr Knox's wife and probes it by reflecting back the feelings in Mr Knox's statement: 'Your wife
would like to see you getting promotion.' This leads the conversation to the effect on husbands of women's desire to gain
prestige in the eyes of their neighbours, culminating in Mr
Stewart's question as to the reaction of Mr Knox's wife to his
promotion within the work study department and Mr Knox's
recognition that this would be likely to solve 'her problem'.
In other words, he sees that the real problem is at least as
much his wife's as his own and that a significant part of his
problem is coming to terms with his wife's ambitions for him,
for the children and for herself. Mr Knox has not simply a
problem at work; he has also got a problem at home, and perhaps a more important one as far as his future happiness is
concerned.

One thing that becomes evident is that with the skilled
interviewer the respondent may feel able to reveal more
deeply held feelings which he may previously have refused
to acknowledge. This places a burden of responsibility upon
the interviewer, in regard to what he says and to what he
does. Of course these feelings are more likely to be revealed

in a counselling interview rather than in a problem-solving one; nevertheless they may occur. The problem-solving interviewer's main task, as we emphasized in chapter one, is not intended to be therapeutic; therefore he must be careful in deciding how far he will allow the respondent to reveal himself. It is not his business to engage in a lengthy series of interviews in an attempt to help the respondent reorientate his total attitude to life. In so far as it is his objective to help him understand himself, it is primarily that he may be able to help him deal with a particular problem. On the other hand the respondent, faced with an understanding person who is prepared to listen to him, may try to use the interviewer as a counsellor and deepen the relationship between them. This is a situation the problem-solving interviewer must treat with great care. If, in his judgement, the respondent needs therapeutic help, he may suggest where and how this is to be obtained. If the respondent is simply craving attention, the interviewer will not have time to offer this, nor will he allow the respondent to become dependent on him. The interviewer will also refuse to allow himself to be cajoled into giving 'good advice'. This is to take the respondent's problem and solve it for him instead of enabling him to solve it for himself. In the end this can mean the respondent comes to rely on the interviewer's judgement instead of being able to make his own judgement; it leaves him even less self-sufficient than he was before. And, if things go wrong, he can blame the advice-giver and escape responsibility for his actions. The more difficult task of standing with the respondent as he sees more clearly the nature of his problem and his own resources for dealing with it and makes his first tentative steps to solve it demands a higher degree of skill on the part of the interviewer. But if the interviewer can manage to accomplish it, the respondent is left a more complete and adequate person because he has learned how to solve the problem for himself. To this extent the interviewer acts therapeutically.

Probing takes place not simply to solve the problem but to enable the respondent to solve it. Only when the interviewer fully accepts the implications of this can he justify the use of his skill to probe; for this is to respect the human dignity of the respondent and does not allow the interviewer to see him merely as an object of interest.

Giving advice can be appropriate in certain factual situations, that is, when the advice is basically informative. The respondent may want to know, for example, the best way to apply for legal assistance or to obtain a mortgage or to put in for a wage increase, and so on. The interviewer may be able to advise him on these things or, at least, to direct him to where he may obtain such advice. But on the underlying problems of whether the respondent should go ahead with a legal action or buy a particular house or apply for more money for the job he is doing, he should be left to make his own decision and not permitted to rely on the interviewer. Advice may be interpreted as instruction, and if the interviewer advises him to take a certain course of action the respondent may well interpret this as an instruction to do so. In fact, whether or not the respondent should do these things is his own responsibility, and for the interviewer to attempt to make the decision instead of leading the respondent to the point where he can make it for himself is neither wise nor is it morally justifiable. In the first case the interviewer will be blamed if the decision turns out to be the wrong one, and in the second the respondent is permitted to become dependent on the interviewer's judgement instead of on his own.

VII. EMBARRASSING TOPICS

At any point during the interview, and especially in probing, topics may arise embarrassing either to the respondent or the interviewer or both. The interviewer has to be sensitive enough to recognize when the respondent is embarrassed and does not wish to pursue some particular theme. Often, however, the less experienced interviewer may become embarrassed by something that does not worry the respondent at all. This causes him to handle the interview badly; the respondent may react defensively and *rapport* may quickly break down.

Interviewer embarrassment happens because we allow our biases to affect the situation; we cease to be objective, we fail to accept. The interview breaks down because we have failed as interviewers; we have ceased to be 'unshockable'. Jung (1933) has written about this, in regard to doctor interviewers: 'It might be supposed that it is easy for the doctor to show understanding in this respect. But people forget that even doctors have moral scruples, and that certain patients' confessions are hard even for a doctor to swallow. Yet the patient does not feel himself accepted unless the very worst in him is accepted too.' He adds: 'We cannot change anything unless we accept it. Condemnation does not liberate, it oppresses.' The embarrassment of the interviewer is in a sense a condemnation of the respondent. It is in effect saying to him: 'I cannot bring myself to talk about this aspect of your behaviour because it is repugnant to me.' Thus the respondent is rejected as a person. He is no longer able to feel that he can reveal the truth about himself and his situation, for the interviewer has ceased to understand him, has ceased to treat him as a person of intrinsic worth. This kind of situation may arise not only in counselling interviews but in problem solving or even in selection-type interviews. For example, in an interview in which a young woman was discussing her child's problems at school, she said: 'In a way I'm more worried about my husband than I am about the boy. He is far more upset than Cecil is.' 'Why is that, do you think?' asked the interviewer. 'Well, the other boys shout things at Cecil because he is coloured and my husband feels this very much.' 'You mean your child is coloured?' asked the interviewer, somewhat taken aback. 'Well yes. You see my husband comes from

72

Trinidad and of course it's from him the boy takes his colour so he feels sort of responsible about it. I think he still finds it odd being married to me though we've been married nine years. He's a bit sensitive. Funny, isn't it, after all this time?'
The interviewer seemed to find it difficult to continue the discussion, let alone ask the kind of questions which would have helped to open up an understanding of the husband's attitudes towards colour, his son, his white wife and himself. The interview petered out and the respondent went away without having been helped to think through her problem or to decide what action might be best to help resolve the situation. Afterwards the interviewer said: 'I was shocked. And she was such a nice-looking girl too.'

Embarrassment is an emotional reaction which has got out of hand. The interviewer who shows embarrassment has lost control of his bias and is unable to prevent showing it in his behaviour. The only remedy consists of first recognizing our bias and then coming to terms with it. As we said before, the interviewer must know a good deal about himself and his own attitudes before he can begin to know very much about other people and theirs.

VIII. ENCOURAGEMENT

In contrast to the stultifying effect on the interview of a display of embarrassment by the interviewer, the interviewer can help the interview forward by encouraging remarks and gestures. The nod of the head to show understanding, the smile, even the deliberate 'Mm hmm' all enable the respondent to feel he is being accepted and encouraged to talk freely. *Psychotherapy* (1965) reported an investigation at the Oregon University Medical School on the effects of the interviewer's use of the response 'Mm hmm'. Forty men who were applying for jobs in the Civil Service were each given a 45-minute interview. During the interviews given to twenty of the men, the interviewer deliberately used the response 'Mm hmm' at frequent intervals in the middle 15-minute period of the interview. Results showed that, in this second period, the respondents in the interviews where this tactic was adopted talked significantly more than during the first and third periods of the interview. In the control interviews given to the twenty other men and in which the interviewer did not use the response 'Mm hmm', there was found to be no significant difference in the amount of respondent talk between the three periods. The investigators concluded that the frequent use by the interviewer of the phrase 'Mm hmm' encouraged the respondent to participate more fully in the conversation. People seem always more ready to talk to someone who makes it evident that he is listening with interest and understanding.

Centers (1963) carried out a somewhat similar investigation with 49 subjects on the effects of simple verbal reinforcements such as 'Yes', 'I see', 'Uh huh', etc. Each subject was instructed by the experimenter to wait for him in the lobby of the psychological laboratory. While he waited, a colleague of the experimenter—who looked and behaved like another subject—came up and began to talk with him, pretending that he also was waiting for the arrival of the experimenter. The conversation was recorded by means of concealed microphones. Eventually, after half an hour, the experimenter arrived and explained to the subject what had been taking place. During the apparently casual conversation, the experimenter's colleague had attempted to manipulate the behaviour of the subject by means of social reinforcement. Areas he had tried to affect were: (a) the total amount of verbalization, (b) statements conveying some information, (c) statements conveying opinion and belief, and (d) questions. Before the colleague administered the reinforcement, the rate at which the subject spoke, conveyed information, expressed opinions and asked questions was measured for ten minutes. A second 10-minute period was given over to measuring the effect of the reinforcement while the last 10-minute period was devoted to extinction training, that is, all positive reinforcement was withdrawn and the experimenter's colleague either remained silent or actively disagreed with the subject. Measurements were carried out by an examination afterwards of the recorded conversations.

Before reinforcement, that is, for the first 10-minute period of the conversation, the average number of verbalizations made by the subjects was 26; this consisted of 11 informative statements, 7 statements of opinion or belief and 8 questions. In the second 10-minute period when reinforcement took place as the experimenter's colleague used the phrases 'Yes', 'I see', etc., verbalizations increased to 38, consisting of 19 informative statements, 13 opinion statements and 6 questions. In the extinction period, verbalization decreased to 5·5, consisting of 2·5 informative statements, 2 opinion statements and 1 question. It is claimed by Centers that the kind of social reinforcement used resulted in considerable changes in the amount of conversation by the subjects. All the types of verbal behaviour, when reinforced, except the questions, showed significant increases over the subjects' normal level and all again decreased significantly during the extinction period when the reinforcement was withdrawn.

IX. A COMMON LANGUAGE—USING WORDS

The interview can go awry when interviewer and respondent get at cross purposes because they misunderstand each other's language. It is important that the interviewer makes sure that the respondent knows precisely what the questions mean and that he understands what is being said to him in reply. 'I'm an amateur ecclesiologist,' said a respondent in reply to a question about his interests. The interviewer had the good sense to say, 'I'm sorry but I didn't quite get that word.' Of course it is not simply that one may use words which his partner in the conversation does not understand; it is that one may use words which allow the other to think that he understands when in fact he fails to do so. We tend to assume that others know what we mean because we use familiar words. Sometimes however the very familiarity of the words disguises the fact that they obscure, rather than reveal, what we are trying to say. Language, our most effective form of communication, has got in the way of communication.

We probably know the story of the young Englishman who was invited to stay with an American family. Impressed by the friendly nature of their hospitality he told his host that he thought his wife was indeed a very 'homely' person, in English a compliment but in American a far from flattering remark. Differences in the meanings attached to words occur not only from country to country but from region to region, from social class to social class, from age group to age group. The interviewer must make sure that the respondent understands what he means—perhaps by phrasing the same question in different ways—and he must make certain that he understands what the respondent says to him. Clarifying questions are of use here: 'Do I take it that your next step is to consult your solicitor?'; 'You mean that you are thinking quite seriously about going to live in New Zealand?'; 'What you're saying is that you feel your marriage is beyond repair?' Specific questions like these go some way to ensure that communication is really taking place.

Communication can also break down because both interviewer and respondent make unwarranted assumptions about the meaning of what they say. We sometimes hear two people carrying on a conversation which appears to make sense and yet in which each later realizes that the other was talking about something different from what he imagined. A simple example is when Mr A, discussing his continental holiday with his friend Mr B, mentions that he saw some serious road accidents in France. He goes on to talk about his holiday but

Mr B assumes he is still talking about motoring accidents while Mr A assumes that Mr B is aware he is in fact discussing holidays abroad. The conversation might proceed like this:

A. I suppose we've come to regard them as a normal part of life.
B. Maybe. More's the pity. There are far too many people being involved in them these days.
A. Oh, that's an exaggeration. They still affect only a limited number of people.
B. Even so, it's far too many. I think the Government should take a much stronger line to try to keep them under control.
A. Surely we've got enough Government interference as it is. People must be left some freedom.
B. What. To be purely destructive.
A. Oh come, it hasn't that effect on the economy. And it broadens the mind; it's an educational experience as well as enjoyable.
B. Road accidents? Are you mad?
A. No, holidays abroad. Aren't we talking about holidays abroad?

These two people, although apparently in communication, are not communicating at all. Each man has made the incorrect assumption that the other is talking about the same thing that he is. The final specific question, 'Aren't we talking about holidays abroad?' is needed to clear up the misunderstanding. It is important for the interviewer to realize the need to summarize from time to time and to check on what the respondent has said as well as to make sure the respondent understands what he is saying, if communication is to be firmly established and maintained.

X. RECORDING THE INTERVIEW

The making of notes during an interview faces interviewers with problems. It means taking their eyes off the respondent and this, many feel, leads to a loss of *rapport.* Some interviewers feel that the respondent is held back from speaking as freely as he might by the fear that everything he says is being noted. Some feel that by having to concentrate on writing down some statement that has been made a moment or two previously, they may lose the thread of the conversation, miss a significant remark or look or gesture. All these are real problems, and so some interviewers prefer to write down the gist of the interview after the respondent has gone. The danger here is that bias may once again help to produce errors of recall.

In his classic book *Remembering,* Sir Frederick Bartlett (1932) points out that both learning and remembering are considerably influenced by the process of *interpreting,* by what he calls 'rationalizing' or the 'effort after meaning'. We tend to interpret events so as to make them 'fit' into our own 'frame of reference'. We do not therefore always remember what really happened; we interpret what happened and remember that. And it seems the longer we take between experiencing the event and recording our memory of it, the more we tend to distort it by the degree of interpretation we make. Bartlett carried out an investigation with some students, using an American folk tale called 'The War of the Ghosts', an unusual story from a very different culture from that of the students' and introducing an element of the supernatural. The students were asked to read the story and then, after various intervals of time, to reproduce it. Bartlett's conclusions are that in such recollection: '1. There will be much general simplification, due to the omission of material that appears irrelevant, to the construction gradually of a more coherent whole, and to the changing of the unfamiliar into some more familiar counterpart. 2. There will be persistent rationalization, both of a whole story and of its details, until a form is reached which can be readily dealt with by all the subjects belonging to the special social group concerned. This may result in considerable elaboration. 3. There will be a tendency for certain incidents to become dominant, so that all the others are grouped about them.' Bartlett's experiment shows that our memories of events are likely to be (a) shortened, and (b) made more coherent by the dropping out of incidents which do not easily fit into the larger pattern.

We have already noticed that in the study made by Guest (1947), the most frequent errors were all basically in the areas of inadequate probing and recording of free responses. In the fifteen interviews, there were noted fifty-three instances where interviewers failed to record 'side comments' or left out parts of a free response which were needed for the proper interpretation of what the respondent said. These 'side comments' created difficulty for the interviewer in that they did not seem to fit the picture which he had begun to build up of the respondent's attitudes. So he left them out altogether or, in a number of instances, changed the wording slightly so that they could fit more closely into the pattern he had begun to build. Accurate recording of the interview is a highly complex skill which may be influenced by bias. Watson and Hartmann (1939) studied the ability of theistic and atheistic students to recall material confirming or denying the existence of God. Most of the results were not statistically significant, nevertheless the writers concluded that their results 'consistently buttress these conclusions, i.e. that material which supported the subjects' attitudinal frame was retained better than material which opposed it'. We have also noted already the experiment carried out by Smith and Hyman (1950) in which a respondent had been instructed to take a position on one question inconsistent with those he took on others. Only one fifth of the interviewers coded the inconsistent response

79

correctly. The others seemed to have a bias to produce a nice consistent pattern even at the expense of accuracy.

It seems then that, if we want to remember an interview accurately, some degree of note taking is likely to be helpful though bias has been shown to affect even the recording of material during the course of the interview. At least there is more chance of accurate recollection if notes have been taken at the time than if we rely simply on our memories after the event. But what about the break in *rapport* that taking our eyes off the respondent might seem likely to bring about? In recent years, some work has been done on the effect of eye contact and the direction of gaze on conversation behaviour. Argyle (1967) states that when two people are engaged in conversation they look each other in the eye intermittently. Each partner in the conversation tends to look at the other between thirty and sixty per cent of the time. He tends to look at the end of any utterance he makes in order to obtain feed-back on the other's response. He tends not to look at the other while he is himself speaking, especially if he is fumbling for the right words with which to express himself. This is presumably so that he will not be distracted by extra information while he is planning and organizing his message. This hypothesis is borne out by the fact that when one of the speakers does look at the listener while he is speaking, he usually speaks fairly fast and fluently. He can afford to look at the listener at this point because he is not having to search for appropriate words to convey his message. People do not however like to be stared at because this seems to convey not interest but the feeling that they are objects. Argyle says that, although eye gaze is satisfying, it is unpleasant and embarrassing if there is too much of it and if mutual glances are too long. These investigations would suggest that (1) the interviewer ought not to attempt to look at the respondent throughout the whole of the interview, but that (2) there are appropriate moments when he should look, for example when he asks a question and the respondent is about to make his response. This means that, if notes have to be taken, they may be taken best at the end of the respondent's statement and before or during the opening words of the interviewer's next question. Of course this means that notes must be very brief.

In many problem-solving interviews, note taking of any sort will be quite out of the question, especially in those that take place unexpectedly and in informal surroundings or where the respondent is clearly emotionally upset. Where the emotional factor does not dominate the interview and when the interview takes place in an office or study where it is possible for the interviewer to have pen and paper unobtrusively to hand, note taking can be very useful as a help to the memory. Even then however it must be used with discretion. It is not permissible to make a verbatim report of all that is said; *rapport* is bound to suffer. It is a matter rather of taking an occasional note here and there of responses that seem to be especially significant and which the interviewer feels it may be important for him to remember accurately. Some explanation of what he is doing may be useful, for example, 'Now that is interesting. Do you mind if I just make a note of that?' or 'That is pretty important. I think we should just get that down on a piece of paper.' Half a dozen key sentences may be of tremendous value in enabling the content of an interview to be recalled accurately while half a dozen pages of notes may have meant the *rapport* was broken and attitudes in consequence scarcely revealed. I have noticed too that, when profuse notes have been taken, they have tended to be almost wholly on a factual level as though the respondent had been discouraged by the sight of so much note taking from willingness to discuss his attitudes.

XI. TERMINATION OF THE INTERVIEW

It is important not to allow the interview to drag on and on with the consequent possibility of its becoming a conversation about nothing in particular and thus ceasing to be an interview. It may be wiser at the beginning of the interview to allocate a time to it but this must obviously be realistic. We have already looked at the example of the interviewer who said, 'I think I can give you ten minutes' and thereby precluded any possibility of the respondent being willing to discuss his attitudes at any depth. If as the interview proceeds it becomes clear that the respondent is going to need more time than the interviewer can give him on this occasion, it is best to make arrangements for the respondent to return later or on another day, depending of course on the urgency of the respondent's need. A short interview now might be of more use than a longer one later but only if the respondent must have some help towards solving his problem quickly; even then a second interview to discuss the situation further will probably be advisable.

It is always important that the respondent be able to go away at the end of the interview knowing what is to happen next: for example, either that he is to return at a set time on an arranged day for a further interview, or that he is to take some specific action or what he is to do if he wishes to meet the interviewer again. If the respondent goes away with no idea of what his next step should be, any useful purpose served by the interview itself may be largely defeated.

To Summarize:

The commencement of a good problem-solving interview is marked by the establishment of adequate *rapport* and the clarification of the interview objective; its termination is marked by checking that the respondent knows what action he should take to deal effectively with his problem and how to make contact again with the interviewer if he should wish to do so.

The interviewer has the task of being at once permissive and systematic, making sure that the respondent is encouraged to talk freely and yet not to wander into irrelevancies but to deal systematically with each aspect of his problem. The interviewer must remember that he is dealing with a complex human being who demands respect and consideration; it is not the interviewer's right to attempt to manipulate him into making a decision that happens to be convenient to him or to the organization he represents or even one that he may sincerely believe to be in the respondent's best interests. He is simply to enable the respondent to see his problem more clearly so that he may himself come to a more informed and therefore probably more adequate decision about the way he should handle it than he would otherwise have done. The intrusion of his own bias will render it impossible for the interviewer to help him do this. Leading questions and evaluative remarks are therefore to be strictly avoided.

At every stage of the interview, the interviewer has to attempt to relate attitudes and behaviour. It is not enough to assume the respondent holds certain attitudes because he says so; the interviewer must probe to discover behaviour which will validate the respondent's claims. Again, the interviewer must probe into behavioural situations described by the respondent to discover what attitudes lie behind them. Skill in using general questions rather than specific ones and in 'reflecting' feelings is essential if the interviewer is to be competent, as is also the capacity to deal objectively with the potentially embarrassing topic, to encourage the respondent to feel the interviewer is listening with understanding and to use words and phrases that facilitate communication.

CHAPTER SIX

The Shape of the Interview

The interviewer has the task of being at once *systematic* and *permissive*, that is, of directing the conversation so that all the key areas relevant to the respondent's problem situation are fully explored and the conversation does not drift into irrelevancies, while at the same time allowing the respondent to feel he is not being prevented in any way from saying all the things he wants to say or looking at areas that seem important to him. At the end of the interview, both interviewer and respondent should feel satisfied with it, the one because through it he has been given all the information which the respondent seems capable of giving concerning his problem, the other because he has been helped to talk as much as he has felt necessary about all the things that seem to him to have contributed in any way to his problem.

If the interview is to be effective, the interviewer must *first* see that its *main objective* is made clear. Both he and the respondent must know exactly why they are engaged in conversation. If the interviewer has initiated the conversation, he will know from the beginning why he has asked the respondent to see him and will have to explain this to him, for example, 'I wanted to talk with you about the new training programme.' If however the interview has been initiated by the respondent, the interviewer will not necessarily know in advance what the interview is to be about or why it has been asked for. His first task in the interview then becomes to discover and state its purpose. This may mean asking 'What have you come to see me about?' or 'Would you like to tell

me why you have asked for this interview?' Until the purpose
of the interview has been clarified, an interview simply cannot take place. It is important that the interviewer be quite
clear about it; he may find it necessary to check that he has
got it right. For example, he may have to say something like,
'So you have come to see me because you feel you'd like
some help in deciding whether or not to take this job overseas?'

The *second* task facing the interviewer is to work out what
specific areas it is necessary to explore with the respondent if
the interview's objective is to be achieved. If the interviewer
has some information beforehand about the problem the interview is likely to be concerned with, he can prepare a tentative
plan, though he may well find he has to change it considerably as the interview proceeds. If, on the other hand, he is not
aware of its objective until the interview is actually under
way, he will have to decide the areas for investigation as he
goes along, picking up significant statements from the respondent and exploring them carefully and in detail. Almost
certainly he will find that he has followed a number of false
trails and that some of the areas which he may look at with
great care do not in fact help the respondent towards a constructive approach to his problem. At least he has eliminated
them for the respondent who now sees that he must turn to
other areas. Each area will be concerned with facts and attitudes; the respondent must be helped to disentangle the facts
from the attitudinal 'frames of reference' which surround
them so that he can assess them for what they really are. We
have seen in chapter five some of the skills needed to accomplish this.

The interviewer's *third* task is to help the respondent, once
he has begun to perceive his problem in new ways, to envisage
a *constructive approach* to it. It must be the respondent who
envisages the approach, not the interviewer, for this alone will
make it fully acceptable to him. The new approach may not

85

always be a full solution of the problem; it may be no more than the creation of a new attitude which means simply the readiness to live with his problem without being overwhelmed by it. It always means however a new way of handling the problem which is a better way than the old one because it has been deliberately thought through and consciously accepted. Each possible approach suggested by the respondent must be looked at in detail with the help of the interviewer's questions. The very fact that the respondent has found someone ready to take time to listen to him seems very often to release his own creative thinking so that he begins to envisage more potential approaches to his problem than he could do when considering it on his own. Sidney and Brown (1961) claim that 'The manager who can listen to his staff, who is prepared to understand their point of view before he does anything else, finds that this action alone is often enough to dispel frustration and to release the speaker's own abilities to handle the problem.'

The interviewer's job is not to evaluate suggested approaches but to ask the kind of questions which will enable the respondent to make his own evaluation. For example, a respondent who is uncertain about promotion prospects in his job may suggest that he might do better overseas. The interviewer is not to say that this is either a good or bad course to follow but to look with him at all the implications of taking a job abroad: How would it affect his family? What differences would it make to his children's education? For how many years would he wish to remain abroad? What would be his position if he eventually decided to return to England? What health hazards might affect him and his family? What about dependent relatives in this country? These and a multiplicity of other questions relevant to the problem would need to be looked at by the respondent before he could make a definite decision about his future. It is not the interviewer's business to answer such questions or even to evaluate the respondent's answers; it is his business only to ask them or to draw the respondent's attention to them.

When the respondent has come to a decision in favour of one particular approach, the interviewer still makes no attempt to evaluate. This is not because he does not care what the respondent does or possesses no values of his own by which to measure the decision, but simply because, if he is to respect the human dignity of the respondent, he must in no sense attempt to make his decision for him. He will already have discussed all the implications of this decision, as of all the other suggestions that have been made, so that the respondent knows precisely what his decision is likely to lead to. Even if he does not approve of the respondent's proposed course of action, whether for moral reasons or for reasons which he regards as 'plain common sense', he must accept the fact that, even when he has faced all the implications of his proposed action, the respondent still wishes to go ahead with it and that it is the respondent's right to do so. In the long run, the respondent must be responsible for his own action; the interviewer cannot accept that responsibility for him. One person cannot live another person's life for him; but he can help him to think out the consequences of his actions, and this the interviewer in fact does.

The *fourth* task for the interviewer is to help the respondent who has decided on a new way in which to approach his problem to work out precisely how he is to put this into effect, in other words, to enable him to work out an *appropriate course of action*. Again it is a matter of asking questions about all the possible ways in which he might act to achieve his chosen approach to the problem rather than proffering advice, however good. The interviewer must see that the respondent comes to an informed decision about the steps to take on leaving the interview.

The interviewer's *fifth* task, which of course permeates the whole of the interview, is to use *appropriate questions and*

87

behaviour. He may define the main objective of the interview, he may investigate all the areas relevant to the problem situation, but if he is unable to decide what questions are appropriate and to couch them in language which is understood by the respondent, he will not be able to fulfil his interviewing role effectively enough to help the respondent envisage a constructive approach to his problem and decide on an appropriate course of action by which to implement it. We have already looked at the skills needed by the interviewer—the capacity to ask general questions, to avoid 'leading' questions, to reflect the respondent's feelings accurately, to probe significant remarks, to be silent when silence is called for so that the respondent may have time to articulate his thoughts accurately, to encourage when encouragement is needed to help the respondent feel that he is being understood, that he is accepted as a person. We have noted the helpful bits of behaviour which the interviewer may perform—his introduction of himself if that is needed, making sure that the interview is not interrupted by phone calls or messages brought in by his secretary, and so on. All these things contribute to the smoothness of the interview and enable the respondent to leave feeling that he has been treated with courtesy and consideration.

In a problem-solving interview, a respondent will make a series of statements involving (1) facts, and (2) attitudes. Sometimes his responses will be concerned with facts alone but often they will be a mixture of both factual and attitudinal material and he may find it difficult to disentangle the two. We have already seen that each of us perceives his world through his own attitudinal 'frame of reference'. This means that while the interviewer will use some behaviour designed specifically to elicit facts, for example the question, 'So it was really your wife who decided to send the children to boarding school?', and other behaviour designed specifically to elicit attitudes, for example the question, 'How did you feel about

88

this?, the question on facts may bring about an attitudinal response as well as a factual one. For example the question, 'So it was really your wife who decided to send the children to boarding school?' may elicit the response, 'Yes, that is correct. But I've regretted it ever since'—which contains both factual and attitudinal material.

Responses such as these are all positive in the sense that they give the interviewer relevant information and so help the interview to move forward towards the achievement of its objective. There are however responses which may be characterized as negative in that they actively get in the way of the interview's achievement of its objective. Responses which are defensive, angry, frustrated or the like come into this group. Responses may be characterized then as (1) indicative of facts and/or attitudes, and (2) positive or negative in so far as they help forward or actively hinder the achievement of the objective of the interview.

As the problem-solving interviewer's intention is to explore both the facts and the attitudes involved in the problem situation, he will use behaviour designed to elicit information about both facts and attitudes. As his task is to enable the respondent to understand his problem situation and devise a constructive approach to it, he will want to obtain positive responses only. Positive responses will be elicited by the interviewer who (a) asks appropriate specific and general questions, (b) reflects attitudes accurately, (c) accepts and reassures the respondent. Negative responses will be elicited by the interviewer who (a) asks inappropriate specific and general questions, (b) reflects attitudes inaccurately, (c) criticizes or argues or shows embarrassment or otherwise exhibits his biases, (d) rejects the respondent.

Sooner or later the interviewer, however competent, is likely to ask a question or use a piece of behaviour which elicits a negative response. How quickly the interview will recover from the breakdown that is threatened depends on how

89

quickly the interviewer responds to the 'feed-back' that is supplied by the angry response or the annoyed look of the respondent, how quickly he diagnoses his error and substitutes a more appropriate question or piece of behaviour and, of course, on how well he has established *rapport* with the respondent in the earlier part of the interview. The respondent may forgive one or two errors on the part of the interviewer but he who goes on making mistakes in the end makes *rapport* impossible and the interview breaks down completely. To ask appropriate questions and use appropriate behaviour is essential if the interview is to survive, let alone lead to a constructive approach to the respondent's problem being devised and worked out.

We may summarize the five tasks of the interviewer in giving an appropriate shape to the interview, as follows:

1. To establish the interview's objective;
2. To decide what specific areas require investigation;
3. To help the respondent envisage a constructive approach to his problem situation;
4. To work out with the respondent an appropriate course of action to achieve his new approach;
5. To use appropriate questions and behaviour throughout the course of the interview.

CHAPTER SEVEN

Analyses of Three Interviews

We shall start with two versions of the same interview situation, the one ineffective because it fails to reveal the respondent's real feelings about the situation, the other effective because it succeeds not only in bringing out the respondent's feelings but in helping her to envisage a more constructive approach to the situation and take appropriate action to implement it. Each interview involves a Miss Endacott, a young shorthand typist, and her boss—in the first interview a Mr Howard, in the second a Mr Burrows.

FIRST INTERVIEW: MR HOWARD INTERVIEWS MISS ENDACOTT

1. Ah, Miss Endacott, do come in. Sit down. I understand you want to see me.
2. Yes, Mr Howard. I've come to hand in my notice.
3. Your notice. But surely this is a bit sudden. I mean, you've only been with us—what is it—less than a year, and I understood you were getting on well and enjoying your job.
4. Well . . . I felt I wanted to make a change.
5. A change? After less than a year?
6. It's not just that exactly. It's that . . . well, I want a job with more money too.
7. But Miss Endacott, you know that you come up for a salary review at the end of your first year with us. I know that Miss Henderson, your supervisor, has told you all about this.

8. Yes, I did know. But ... well, you see, it isn't just the money either. It's the travelling time. I find it awkward getting here.
9. Oh come, Miss Endacott. Lots of the girls have more difficult journeys than you.
10. Well, even so, I want a job nearer home.
11. So you've found a job with more money and less effort to get there. Well, I can only say I'm very disappointed. We've gone to a lot of trouble training you and you leave after such a short time. It seems to me you have never really given the job a chance.
12. I'm sorry, Mr Howard, but that isn't true. I think I've worked as hard as any of the girls while I've been here.
13. I didn't mean to imply that you hadn't. I'm only saying that it seems a great pity you walk out on us like this.
14. I'm not walking out on you, Mr Howard. I'm entitled to leave on a week's notice and I'm handing in my proper notice.
15. I see. Well, today is Friday. So you want to leave next Friday?
16. Yes please.
17. All right. I'll see that everything is made ready for you. Does your new firm require a reference from us?
18. Well, I ... I expect they'll let me know.
19. All right then, Miss Endacott.
20. Thank you, Mr Howard. May I go now?
21. Of course. Goodbye, Miss Endacott, and I can only say how sorry I am that you have decided to leave us like this. I hope you'll stay a little longer with your next firm.

SECOND INTERVIEW: MR BURROWS INTERVIEWS MISS ENDACOTT

1. Ah, Miss Endacott, do come in. Sit down. I understand you want to see me.

2. Yes, Mr Burrows. I've come to hand in my notice.
3. Your notice. I'm sorry to hear that. What has happened? Tell me about it.
4. Well . . . I felt I wanted to make a change.
5. Mm hmm.
6. I think I ought to be getting more money.
7. You feel we're not paying you enough.
8. Well, I know I come up for a salary review at the end of my first year here. Miss Harrison told me about it. But . . . well, it's the expense of getting here as well. It costs quite a lot. And it takes a long time. I really want a job nearer home.
9. You feel we are rather far away.
10. Yes, I do really. And the buses are so awful. You never know how long you're going to have to wait. It's so awkward.
11. So you'd like to make a move?
12. Yes. I've decided to look for another job.
13. And have you found one yet?
14. Well, not yet. But I'll be all right. I'll get one next week, I expect. I won't have any trouble.
15. No, I'm sure not. Miss Harrison has told me what a hard worker you are.
16. Miss Harrison. Oh?
17. You sound surprised.
18. Well, I didn't think she'd noticed what I did.
19. I see.
20. I'm sorry if that sounds rude. I shouldn't have said it. I didn't really mean to.
21. But you felt she didn't notice your work?
22. Not really. I mean . . . well, I hadn't intended to say anything about it but I did feel I was overlooked for the job in Mr Fox's office.
23. Why was that, Miss Endacott?
24. It was Miss McGregor's job. When I heard she had to go

93

back to Scotland to look after her father, I thought I had a chance of being considered at least. I even mentioned it to Miss Harrison. She said she'd see what she could do. Then the next thing I heard was that Miss Barwell had got the job. And I've been here longer than she has.

25. You were disappointed?

26. Yes, I was. I thought at least I might have been considered. Or given an interview. But nobody even talked to me about it. And Miss Harrison never said another word and I'd been relying on her.

27. You hoped she would have put your name forward?

28. Yes. I don't want to suggest that I think I *ought* to have been given the job but I do think I should have been considered for it . . . given an interview for it maybe. Particularly as I had talked to Miss Harrison about it.

29. And Miss Harrison never explained to you why Miss Barwell was given the job?

30. No, she didn't. Anyway, it doesn't matter now.

31. Still, I think you ought to know. Unfortunately Miss McGregor had to go off at very short notice—she had quite a crisis to attend to at home—so she had no time to train a successor. It so happened that Miss Barwell had helped Miss McGregor for a couple of months last year— you may remember that—and so she had quite a good idea of how the office worked. Because of this, Mr Fox asked if she might take over and we agreed.

32. So it wasn't because she was better than me?

33. It was a matter of convenience really. Though, mind you, Miss Barwell is doing a very good job.

34. Of course. But that means there was nothing personal in it after all.

35. You thought there had been? ·

36. Well, I thought that maybe Miss Harrison had said that I . . . that I wasn't really suitable. Particularly as she didn't say anything about it afterwards.

37. Oh no. Miss Harrison has already put in your recommendation for your salary increase. And a very good report on you too.
38. Oh dear, I am sorry ... I mean not about the increase ... or the report. I mean for thinking so badly of her. Though she might have told me about Miss Barwell.
39. No doubt she meant to. She's been awfully busy, you know.
40. I can see that. Mr Burrows, I'm sorry about it all. I've been thinking all sorts of things that I can see now were quite wrong. Do you think I could withdraw my notice please?
41. Well, you haven't actually given it officially yet, you know.
42. Oh. So it's all right then?
43. Of course it is. Perhaps we can just forget about the whole thing, eh?
44. Yes please. And thank you for having been so ... so patient with me, Mr Burrows.
45. I'm so glad you've decided to stay, Miss Endacott ... and I know Miss Harrison will be also. I hope, now that things are straightened out, you'll go on being happy here.
46. I'm sure I shall. Thank you so much, Mr Burrows.

A quick contrast between the two interviews is provided by a comparison of the amounts of interviewer-respondent participation. In the first interview Mr Howard, judging by the number of words used, speaks during sixty-six per cent of the time while Miss Endacott speaks for thirty-four per cent; in the second interview Mr Burrows speaks for slightly less than forty per cent while Miss Endacott speaks for just over sixty per cent. This means that, in the first interview, the interviewer does most of the talking; in the second he does most of the listening.

With the help of the information given in chapter six concerning the five tasks facing an interviewer, we shall try to discover why the first interview went wrong.

1. *Clarifying the Main Objective*
Miss Endacott, in her opening statement, declares her purpose in coming to see Mr Howard: 'I've come to hand in my notice.' Mr Howard does not however attempt to define an objective that he and Miss Endacott can agree on and on which a worthwhile interview could be built. It becomes evident, as the interview proceeds, that his first objective is simply to persuade Miss Endacott to change her mind and withdraw her notice. When this fails he uses the interview as an opportunity to reprimand the girl for her action: '... it seems a great pity you walk out on us like this.' Because Mr Howard has failed to define an objective which both he and Miss Endacott can accept as valid for the interview, neither of them can follow any logical pattern in shaping their discussion.

2. *Deciding on Specific Areas for Investigation*
Failure to define a valid objective makes it impossible for Mr Howard to decide on appropriate areas for investigation. He looks at the two areas in which Miss Endacott claims she is dissatisfied, money and travel time, but does not allow her the opportunity to develop her statements on her attitudes to these two factors to discover how important they really are. He simply tries to resist her attitudes by criticisms which the respondent resists in turn.

3. *Constructive Approach*
Miss Endacott's solution to her problem is simply to hand in her notice, that is, to withdraw from the situation. Mr Howard has been unable to help her make a more constructive approach and so the interview becomes one of recrimination which merely confirms her in her decision.

4. Appropriate Course of Action

In paragraph 17 Mr Howard offers to help Miss Endacott take what action is necessary for her to leave the company. As however her decision to leave does not form a constructive approach to her problem, Mr Howard's behaviour at this point has little positive value.

5. Appropriate Questions and Behaviour

Miss Endacott is pushed on to the defensive right from the beginning of the interview. Mr Howard makes no attempt to understand her attitudes; he simply opposes her decision as unreasonable and she seems to see every comment he makes as some sort of criticism of her behaviour. In the end, he rejects the girl completely (paragraphs 11, 13 and 21). This may ease his own frustration but must simply increase the girl's resentment. It appears that he is not really interested in Miss Endacott but only in solving the problem to his own satisfaction and without taking her feelings into account. At the end of the interview he has as little understanding of her attitudes as he had at the beginning.

Looking at the second interview in the same way as we have looked at the first, let us see if we can now discover why it went so differently and how Miss Endacott was helped by Mr Burrows to make a more constructive approach to her problem.

1. Clarifying the Main Objective

Miss Endacott again states her purpose: 'I've come to hand in my notice.' Mr Burrows is not put out by this but proposes an objective for the interview: 'What has happened? Tell me about it.' This means he sees a purpose for the interview in giving the respondent an opportunity to talk about her decision and discuss her attitudes towards her situation. Unlike Mr Howard, he is not concerned to use the interview as an opportunity to impose his own solution to the problem. He treats Miss Endacott as a person and not a mere hindrance to his own plans. Miss Endacott accepts Mr Burrows's objective as valid and co-operates sufficiently to enable the interview to follow a logical pattern.

2. *Deciding on Specific Areas for Investigation*

Mr Burrows, like Mr Howard, looks at the two main areas in which Miss Endacott professes to be dissatisfied, money and travel time. Unlike Mr Howard, however, he helps her to express her attitudes towards these quite freely so that she is able to go on to say something about her attitudes towards a possible new job. He picks up the significant way in which she refers to Miss Harrison, her supervisor, and again allows her to express her feelings freely. This enables her to state her real problem which is her attitude towards her failure to obtain the job she wanted in Mr Fox's office. He is thus able to provide her with further information about the appointment (paragraph 31) which enables her to create a new attitude towards it.

3. *Constructive Approach*

The creation of this new attitude means that Miss Endacott has been able to make a constructive approach to the situation. She can now accept it without resentment. And she can also adopt a new attitude towards Miss Harrison.

4. *Appropriate Course of Action*

Miss Endacott makes her own decision about what course of action she would like to take (paragraph 40) and Mr Burrows confirms that this is approved (paragraphs 41 and 43).

5. *Appropriate Questions and Behaviour*

Mr Burrows is positive in his behaviour all the way through the interview. He allows Miss Endacott to express her feelings without criticizing or rejecting her in any way; he helps her to feel that she is being understood and accepted so that she is helped to reveal her real reason for wanting to leave (paragraph 22). By the time that Mr Burrows comes to offer her information on a rational level (paragraph 31), she is able to listen and accept it. Mr Burrows goes on to offer her reassurance and encouragement and the interview ends on a positive note when she is able not only to construct a new approach to her situation and decide appropriate action to take but also to thank him for the way he has listened to her.

Mr Burrows must realize that it was wrong of Miss Harrison not to have informed Miss Endacott of what had happened about the appointment. He specifically checks on Miss Harrison's omission (paragraph 29) but makes no attempt to criticize her in front of Miss Endacott and indeed defends her (paragraph 39). One may suspect however that he will have a word with her privately at a convenient moment so that she does not make the same sort of mistake again.

Mr Burrows's objective in the interview is not to try to make Miss Endacott change her total personality; even if such a task were needed, it would not be within his capacity. He is concerned simply to help her find a constructive solution to the problem facing her, but the very fact that he is concerned to help *her* find the solution and not simply to impose his own, as Mr Howard attempted to do, means that he is showing his respect for her as a person and according to her the human dignity she wants, and which indeed she felt the company had denied her in not considering her claim for the vacancy in Mr Fox's office.

We now take another interview, a rather longer one, and use the same technique of analysis. The interview concerns a social worker, employed by a voluntary agency, who wants to talk about the conditions under which she is expected to perform her work. After the opening preliminaries, the interview continues like this:

1. I wanted to talk to you about my job. I'm feeling awfully dissatisfied with it at the moment. I took it on in such a blaze of enthusiasm; it seemed so worth while and so ... well, so right for me. I wouldn't like to think I'd lost my enthusiasm but I've begun to wonder if I'm not just wasting my time. So many things seem to have gone wrong on me.

2. I see. Can you tell me a bit about the job?

3. Well, I work full time, as you know, under the direction of a committee. At least, they don't tell me what to do exactly but they advise about broad principles. I have to report back to them each month and then they talk about that. It's all a bit formal. They don't really interfere. But of course they employ me and they could sack me if they didn't like the way I did the job. I'm the only full-time worker but they've got a number of people who do voluntary work. At least they're supposed to. That's part of the problem really; they're inclined to let things slide.

4. I see.

5. The idea was that they'd take the load of routine work off the back of the full-time worker—you know, things like typing letters and working the office duplicator and seeing that information leaflets went out to all the right places and so on. But I always seem to be kept waiting. They're always late with things or they're making excuses about not doing them at all.

6. What happens then?

7. It usually ends up by my doing overtime to get the things done myself. You know, coming into the office in the evening in my own time to do the duplicating and so on. Or, what's worse, doing it in office hours when I should be getting on with my proper work. I've never suggested I get any money for the overtime work, of course. I've just got on and done it. It's been the only way to keep the work moving. Even so, it still gets behind.

8. You mean that, in spite of all this extra work, you still can't keep up?

9. I'm afraid that's it. There are about a dozen helpers, you see, and I could not hope to do all their work. At least not properly. Even when they do it, I've got to chase them up and that is such a waste of time. They're just . . . quite unreliable.

10. You feel you can't depend on them.

11. No. I cannot understand why they took on the job if they were not prepared to do it. Nobody forced them. They're all friends of the committee members who apparently asked them to help years ago.

12. What sort of people are they exactly? I mean, are they elderly retired people? Or housewives? Or young people?

13. Oh, elderly people actually. And all women. I think they're too old really. When they took on the work originally, I expect it was all right. I imagine their children had just left school or got married or something and they found they had extra time on their hands and wanted to do something useful with it. Of course this kind of work must have seemed just the right thing for them. It was a 'good cause', if you know what I mean. But that was twenty years or more ago. That's when most of them started. But they won't let go; they still hang on. But it's too much trouble for them now. So they're no real help at all.

14. When do they do this work? In your office during the day? Or at home when they've got a free hour or so?

15. They're supposed to come to the office, mostly in the mornings. There's a rota system . . . you know, Mrs Jones is supposed to come in at ten on a Thursday morning and stay till twelve . . . and Mrs Smith to do it on a Friday. But more than half the time they never turn up . . . and don't even ring to explain. Or, if they do come, it's at

ten-thirty and then they make excuses about having to get away early. The whole system is a shambles.

16. Who controls them? Who arranges the rota, for example?

17. Well, I should do. But they won't hear of their times being changed. I had wondered if they might do better if we switched them to the afternoons. It would have been more difficult for me as I'd have had to use the mornings to get out of the office instead of the afternoons. But I'd have tried it if it might have improved things. But they all got quite upset about the idea. Felt I was being critical of them. Well, I was too. They go on about having done this work for years and the last worker was always satisfied and appreciated them. Meaning I don't, I suppose. They seem to think I'm just being awkward. They're always throwing up the merits of the woman who used to do my job.

18. Mm hmm.

19. Well, she did the work all right. But she'd been doing it for twenty years too—just like them. And when she left last year she was still doing it the same way as when she began. She hadn't made a change in years. I want to make changes. I want to try new ways of doing things. The whole work needs broadening and these people just won't see it.

20. You feel they just won't see your point of view.

21. That's it. They're all stuck in the same rut they were in twenty years ago.

22. Have you been able to discuss with them what your new ideas are and how you'd like to develop them?

23. Well, I've said I wanted to make changes. I asked them if they'd like to come in the afternoons instead of the mornings. And that we can only develop if they turn up regularly, and so on.

24. What was their reaction?

25. Oh, the usual stuff about the last worker. She hadn't seen

any need to make changes. What they did was good enough for her. And so on. The old hypocrite.

26. You feel she wasn't sincere.

27. In a way. She came up from the country one day—she's retired down to Sussex—and I had a long talk with her. She told me that she had had lots of problems with the helpers, that they weren't doing the work efficiently. But evidently she had told *them* that they were wonderful, that she could never have managed without them. If she'd had any courage, she'd have got rid of them before she left instead of handing them all over to me to deal with. She as much as admitted it. Said she hadn't wanted any trouble before she went so she never said anything to them. Now I've inherited the problem. And it's a lot harder for me to deal with than it would have been for her. The committee couldn't have avoided listening to her if she'd gone to them about it. She'd been there so long. But oh no, she left it for me. It's bad enough being at loggerheads with the workers; I don't want to run across the committee as well—not at this stage anyway.

28. Are these voluntary workers accountable to the committee?

29. Accountable to the committee? Well, I suppose in theory yes. The committee ought to be able to do something about the situation. But in fact they don't. I don't really think the committee is very effective. But then you know what they are. Nice people who turn up once a month and then forget about the whole affair. There is no one person who is really prepared to be responsible for seeing that things get done . . . well, that isn't quite fair perhaps . . . the chairman is quite helpful . . . or tries to be. He is younger than most of them. But when you're dealing with people who have promised to help you for nothing, I suppose it is difficult to press them too hard. Maybe he feels it better to have inadequate help than none at all.

30. How do you yourself feel?

31. I don't really know. You see, nobody has any real authority over them. You're just dependent on their good graces all the time. So if they don't do the work, you've no alternative but to do it yourself.

32. How much of this did you know before you took on the job?

33. I didn't. The previous worker had been ill and so I didn't meet her until after I'd accepted the job. The chairman gave me most information. It all sounded fine. Then I met the committee and I was quite impressed. I thought they were nice. They are nice too. And the helpers. I met them. Of course they gave me glowing accounts of the work they did to help. And I believed them all. After all, I was just straight out of college and it seemed wonderful to be offered a job like this. I should have known there was a catch. I was a bit obsessed really by all the opportunities I thought I'd have and I just wasn't careful enough in making enquiries.

34. You'll be more careful another time?

35. Indeed I will. I've learned my lesson.

36. Yes. Well now, let's see. Where were we? Ah yes, we were talking about your having to do so much of the work yourself. Isn't that right?

37. Yes. It's a real problem for me.

38. Suppose you lost all the helpers. How would you get the work done then?

39. Well, the committee might get some new helpers, I suppose. That shouldn't be impossible. Some younger and more active people. Or they could perhaps arrange to get the work done at a typing agency. But that would cost money. Not that that ought to be an insuperable difficulty. But because I'm so new I'm a bit hesitant yet about suggesting this. Maybe I shouldn't be. The trouble is that some of them have been on the committee for years.

They're just like the helpers. The work has always jogged along in the past without much effort on their part and they expect it to jog along for ever. I want to make it do better than jog along. I want to make a real advance. I want to extend it and develop it. And I cannot do it until I get proper help.

40. Have you been able to discuss your ideas at all with the committee?

41. Well, I don't know that I've discussed my ideas much with anybody but I've told them I could do with more help. I didn't want to make too much of an issue of it though. Actually, the chairman did promise he would speak to the helpers. But I don't know whether he did or not. Anyway, it has not made any difference so far as I can see.

42. Mm hmm. Do you think the committee could do anything very effective if you could persuade them that your ideas were worth following up?

43. Oh yes. They've got lots of local contacts—I'm more or less a newcomer to the area—and it should not be all that difficult to find some new helpers who would really help. Younger people. Or they could raise enough money to get me a part-time secretary. I'm sure there are lots of house-wives who have some spare time on their hands and who would like to help and would not ask exorbitant wages. Somebody like that coming into the office two or three mornings a week would make a world of difference.

44. Do you think the committee might be receptive to these ideas if you told them how much they matter to you?

45. I think they might. After all, they're a well-meaning group of people. And they must believe the work is worth-while. Otherwise they would not be on the committee at all. There is a job that needs doing. It's just that I think they have never really realized how much work is needed

to get it done properly. So they have never provided the proper resources.

46. You feel they have been a bit unrealistic about the demands of the work.

47. That's right. They employed me to do a job. I want to do it. I am prepared to work hard at it. In fact I am working hard at it. But I do not want to spend my time typing letters or putting circulars in envelopes when I have my real job to get on with. After all, I was trained for this job. It's a skilled job. I've got a degree. It is up to them to help me if they really want it done.

48. How can you best get this across to them?

49. Perhaps I should have a heart to heart talk with the chairman first. As I said, he tries to be helpful. Then perhaps he could put it across to the committee. Or at least back me up if I did.

50. You think he would be willing to do that?

51. I think so. You know, I've probably not taken him into my confidence as much as I should. Or the committee, for that matter. I've just grumbled and tried to deal with the situation myself. I've wasted an awful lot of time going round the helpers or just doing extra work in the evenings. Well, not wasted it exactly ... you know what I mean ... done it when it wasn't really my job to do it. I should have had it all out more thoroughly with the committee. It has been my own fault to some extent, I suppose.

52. You feel you have got to accept some responsibility yourself.

53. I think so. Of course when you are new you hesitate to appear too aggressive. Maybe, now that I'm more settled in, I can be a bit more ... well, demanding.

54. You can ask for a little bit more than you have done.

55. Yes. I think I can put it to them more firmly now that they must accept more responsibility. I can show them

I've tried and simply have not been able to manage. They have got to see that they have as much responsibility as I have for seeing that the work is properly done. Obviously the chairman is the first person for me to tackle about it. I'm sure he has got a special responsibility. After all, he is the chairman.

56. He has really got to help you.

57. Yes. I'll talk it over with him and then we can put it to the committee. Either they will have to provide me with some new helpers who will be effective or raise the extra money to pay for a part-time secretary. If not, I cannot carry on. It's as simple as that really. If I don't get the help I want, I'll resign.

58. You'll tell them this?

59. Well . . . oh, I don't know. Perhaps that would be wrong. It might put their backs up. Make them feel I was threatening them. And I don't want to do that. Anyway, I'm keen on this job and I wouldn't want to walk out on it. I've only been doing it six months and that is such a short time. Especially as it's my first job. It would look bad, wouldn't it, to pack it up so soon? I'd feel a bit ashamed of myself if I did that.

60. Mm hmm.

61. People who did not know the circumstances would think it odd I gave up so quickly. No, I don't think I would be prepared to leave so soon . . . not unless the situation were really desperate. And it's not that. No, I think I've just got to make sure the committee give me the help I need. That's all that's to it.

62. And you think they can manage that?

63. Why not? They have been running the organization on the cheap for years . . . with all these voluntary helpers. They have never set themselves to put the thing on a proper financial basis. They have got so many contacts in this town they ought to be able to draw in more than

enough subscriptions from business people and industry and so on. You need money to run anything effective nowadays. Of course they have always seen themselves as dedicated to a good cause and that therefore people should be glad to help them on a voluntary basis. Well, if they want to serve the good cause, they cannot get by on the kind of voluntary helpers they have got now. One part-time secretary . . . I'm hardly asking the earth.

64. You really feel this would solve your problem?

65. I do. Unless the work expands so much they need another full-time worker like me. It's the sort of thing the State will have to take over in the end, I suppose.

66. The voluntary bodies won't be able to continue to cope.

67. Not really. They haven't the resources. I mean I think the idea of voluntary service and all that is marvellous. If it hadn't existed in the past we'd be missing a lot of good things in society. I'm sure we still need it. But it has got to be properly backed up . . . with proper resources. I mean you couldn't run the educational system that way. Education is so advanced you have got to be prepared to spend hundreds of thousands of pounds to do it properly. Or the hospital service. It's the same with everything, I think.

68. But in the meantime, all you want is one part-time secretary?

69. (laughs) All I want is one part-time secretary.

70. So what do you see yourself doing to get her?

71. Well obviously I've got to have some plain speaking with the committee. Up till now I've just been avoiding it. I suppose I've just got to screw up my courage and get on with it.

72. You feel it will take some courage.

73. Oh, not really. I mean that I'll have to be firm about it . . . make my proposals pretty definitely. I'll tell them what I want to do and explain that the present system is unwork-

able, that we can never build up the organization until we have more effective help and that means finding the money to pay for a secretary.

74. When are you likely to be able to do this?

75. There is a committee meeting next week. But I'll see the chairman first and put it to him and make sure I have got his support. I'm sure it would make all the difference if he were to take a strong line in my favour. Maybe he would even put it to the committee himself.

76. So your next step is to see the chairman?

77. Yes, that's right.

78. Then together you will put it to the committee?

79. That seems to be the best thing. After all, it's their responsibility. I'm only their employee. If they want the job done properly ... and I'm sure they do ... then they have got to do something to provide adequate help for me. I think I've known for some time that I really ought to go to the committee about this but I never seemed to be able to spur myself to do it. In a way, I felt it was like admitting defeat ... saying I couldn't do the job. But I can see I've just got to put it to them.

80. Mm hmm.

81. It's not just my responsibility ... it's theirs too. It's more theirs than mine, in fact. So I really will do something to bring them in on it. ... You know, I am grateful to you for listening to me. I hope you didn't mind.

82. Of course not. Come again some time if you want to. You have only to telephone and we can make an appointment.

83. Thank you. I would like to come round some time and let you know how I get on.

1. *Clarifying the Main Objective*

The interviewer has evidently made it possible in the first part of the interview (not recorded) for the respondent to feel free to define her objective in coming to see him: 'I wanted to talk to you about my job. I'm feeling awfully dissatisfied with it at the moment.' (paragraph 1.) The interviewer accepts this statement without attempting to evaluate it and simply asks for further information. The objective of the interview is thus accepted by both interviewer and respondent as being to discuss the respondent's job and her present dissatisfaction with it.

2. *Deciding on Specific Areas for Investigation*

When he has heard the respondent's description of her work situation, the interviewer is able to select four specific areas for investigation: (a) the respondent's relationship with the committee; (b) her relationship with the voluntary helpers; (c) the relationship of the committee to the voluntary helpers; and (d) the resources necessary for effective performance in the job. From (a) it is learnt that the demands of the committee on the respondent are not realistic, for it expects her to do her work without the provision of adequate resources (paragraphs 45–47). At the same time however the respondent is not herself entirely blameless, for she has not explained to the committee just why she needs this extra help (paragraphs 40–51). Communication between the respondent and her committee is thus seen to be ineffective with the result that the committee has failed to see the need for providing more resources than it provided for the previous worker. (b) Shows that the relationship between the worker and her voluntary helpers is also confused. The quality of her work depends on their co-operation and she is accountable to the committee for this work. Yet she has been given no authority over the helpers. She cannot control their work or dismiss them. She has no financial resources available with which to get the work done in some other way. She points out that the voluntary helpers are 'inclined to let things slide' (paragraph 3); 'They're always late with things or they're making excuses about not doing them at all.' (paragraph 5.) On the other hand, it appears that the respondent in her relationship with her helpers has not done very much to enthuse them as she has failed to tell them anything about her new ideas for enlarging the work (paragraphs 22, 23, 51). There appears to be some evidence that the workers feel they are unappreciated (paragraph 17) and it is certainly true that the respondent is highly critical of them (paragraph 21) so may have displayed her attitude in her dealings with them. This leads to the investigation of (c) the relationship of the committee to the voluntary helpers. In theory these helpers are accountable to the committee (paragraph 29). In practice, nobody seems to hold them to account. If the chairman spoke to them, they apparently took little notice (paragraph 41). The result is that the worker is left to get on with the job as best she can (paragraph 7). Finally (d) the interviewer looks with the respondent at the resources she feels she needs. New voluntary helpers or the use of a typing agency (paragraph 39) or, best of all, a part-time secretary (paragraphs 43, 57, 63, 69) are suggested. The interviewer checks with the respondent that she feels a part-time secretary would seem to her to solve her problem best (paragraph 64) and she assures him that it would (paragraph 65). All this information now opens up the way to the setting up of a constructive approach to the problem.

3. Constructive Approach

The respondent sees that the solution to her problem involves the establishment of a new kind of relationship with the committee: 'They employed me to do a job. . . . It is up to them to help me if they really want it done' (paragraph 47). She has been trying to deal with the problem on her own (paragraph 7) and that has not worked. She now realizes that only the committee has the power to solve the problem effectively for only they can provide her with the resources she needs. So she must go to the committee, put forward her ideas, obtain their approval for them and ask them to give her what she needs.

She must bring them into the picture, involve them in the work (paragraphs 55, 79, 81).

4. Appropriate Course of Action

With a constructive approach to the problem in sight, the interviewer makes sure that the respondent comes to a decision about the steps to take to make it effective (paragraph 70). The respondent accepts that she has got 'to have some plain speaking with the committee' (paragraph 71). The interviewer goes on to check when she will do this and the respondent decides that an appropriate occasion will be the committee meeting the following week (paragraph 75). She decides that, before putting her case to the committee members, she ought first to talk it through with the chairman. The procedure for working this out is planned in paragraphs 76–79.

5. Appropriate Questions and Behaviour

No interview is likely to be faultless and the interviewer here makes a number of errors. In paragraph 32 he asks a question which leads to a digression from the main theme of the interview. He makes rather a banal comment in paragraph 34 but recovers himself by paragraph 36 and goes on to encourage the respondent to envisage alternative ways of dealing with her work load. He goes wrong again however in paragraph 52 when he 'reflects' incorrectly and the respondent at once goes on to the defensive. Fortunately, at this stage in the interview the *rapport* between interviewer and respondent is strong enough to surmount the setback and the respondent goes on to make a positive statement of her plans.

Notice how, at the end of the interview, she is able to thank the interviewer for listening to her. She is able to see him in a supportive role; she has to go ahead and take action herself to deal with her problem but she is left aware that she can come back if she wishes and the interviewer will help her think through her position.

(It will be obvious that this interview has been severely edited in order to shorten and disguise it. The real interview on which it is based lasted more than an hour; as recorded here, it can be read aloud in twenty minutes or so.)

CHAPTER EIGHT

Learning to Interview

No one is likely to imagine that he can learn to interview simply by reading a short book about interviewing. If he is to become a competent interviewer he will need to practise his interviewing skills in real life situations or in role play situations that approximate fairly closely to real life and with the help of an instructor who can discuss his skills with him. This will usually mean attending a course run either by his company or by an outside training organization.

Many people however are already engaged in interviewing and have to make do as best they can without any course of instruction being available to them. While obviously a period of time spent on a group training scheme would be likely to bring about a greater improvement in their performance, they can still make an improvement by applying the principles outlined in this book, by thinking back over the interviews they do conduct (if possible with the aid of notes) and examining them carefully to assess their strengths and weaknesses. Why did the interview 'dry up' at this point? What had I just said to the respondent? Why did the respondent show signs of irritation at being asked this question? How had I phrased it? Could I have phrased it differently? At this point did I cease to interview and begin to argue? If so, why? Was I being influenced by some bias of which I was not aware? Why did I feel annoyance or resentment when the respondent made this particular remark? Is this again evidence of a bias on my part which I have not adequately faced up to? In this part of the conversation did I talk too much and listen too little? What impelled me to do so? Why did I interrupt him here? Why did I express my own views instead of waiting to hear his? What was the question I asked or comment I made that suddenly enabled the respondent to open up and really begin to reveal the roots of his problem? These are all questions that the interviewer needs to ask himself after any interview.

One useful method of obtaining help in assessing one's interviewing skills is to persuade a friend to allow himself to be interviewed and then to discuss frankly with the interviewer the way in which he felt the interview was conducted. If the respondent is sufficiently secure in his friendship with the interviewer to permit the interview to be recorded on tape, a great deal of useful information can be obtained if they analyse it together and try to discover why each said what he did at each point of the interview. The recorded interview can be examined under the five headings we described in chapter six.

There is considerable value too in finding someone with experience in interviewing and asking him to interview the learner and allow the interview to be recorded. The learner is then able to look at his own reactions to the various strategies of the interviewer and in consequence assess them as of positive or negative value. He will find it useful to ask himself such questions as: What did the interviewer say at this point that enabled me to respond more easily? What did he do that brought about this breakdown in the conversation? How did he attempt to re-establish *rapport*? and so on.

While methods like these cannot take the place of the group learning situation, the learner on his own or with the help of a friend can still make a useful improvement in performance if he uses them and also if he cultivates the habit of thinking critically about any interviews he may have to undertake in his working life and applies to them the criteria which this book has described.

We pointed out that, before an interviewer can be sure he

is not biasing an interview situation with his own prejudices, it is necessary for him to understand and come to terms with his own attitudes. Many companies and organizations throughout Western Europe and America have begun to use what are called training or T-groups in an attempt to enable their employees achieve a greater degree of self-understanding. Members of a T-group have no set agenda; they study simply the processes of their own interaction in the group with the assistance of a trainer who observes what goes on and, from time to time, offers interpretations of it. Each member tries to discover how his behaviour is perceived by the other members of the group. This is made possible by the immediate 'feedback' that takes place in the group situation when members of the group discuss the way in which they see the behaviour of one of their number. T-groups take place usually within a residential course of a week or a fortnight although, of recent years, experimentation has taken place with groups that meet at weekly intervals for about two hours on each occasion and over a period of anything from three to twelve months. Bunker (1965), following a study of two hundred people who attended the Bethel Laboratories in the USA, claimed that the trainees changed in various areas including their understanding of the behaviour both of others and of themselves and in their sensitivity to the needs of others. There is evidence however that similar results can be obtained by the less dramatic method of a combination of lectures and group discussion on human relations problems, cf. Sorenson (1958).

Courses more directly concerned with interviewing skills give the opportunity to learn something of one's own biases in the practical sessions when one respondent is interviewed by several course members in succession and the trainees later discuss together the way in which they have perceived the respondent and his attitudes. This provides opportunities for the trainee interviewers to realize if they have failed to come to terms with some respondent who has presented few or no difficulties to their colleagues or if their perception of him is out of line with that of the others. Discussion with each other and with the course tutor may bring to light bias in their approach which they can then begin to deal with.

The trainee interviewer can be best helped in his self-understanding by membership of a T-group or by attendance at a series of lectures and discussions on human relations problems and by a competently run course on interviewing techniques which involves practical exercises in interviewing. But if all this is impossible, then the kind of self-help described in the opening paragraphs of this chapter will make a not inadequate substitute and will enable him to become an interviewer who is at least aware both of the objectives of the interview and of the skills which he must apply to achieve them.

REFERENCES

Allport, G. W., 'Attitudes', in *Handbook of Social Psychology*, ed. C. Murchison, Worcester, Mass.: Clark Univ. Press, 1935.

Argyle, M., *The Psychology of Interpersonal Behaviour*, Penguin Books, 1967.

Bartlett, F. C., *Remembering*, London: C.U.P., 1932.

Benedict, R., *Patterns of Culture*, first edition 1934, Penguin edition 1946.

Bunker, D., 'The Effect of Laboratory Education on Individual Behaviour', in Schein, E. H. and Bennis, W. G. (eds), *Personal and Organizational Change through Group Methods*, N.Y.: Wiley, 1965.

Calahan, D., Tamulonis, V. and Verner, H. W., 'Interviewer Bias Involved in Certain Types of Attitude Questions', *Internat. J. of Opin. and Attitude Research*. I, 63–77, 1947.

Cantrill, H. (ed.), *Gauging Public Opinion*, Princeton Univ. Press, 1944.

Centers, R., A Laboratory Adaptation of the Conversational Procedure for the Conditioning of Verbal Operants, *J. Abnorm. Soc. Psy.* 67, 334–339, 1963.

Charters, W. W. Jr and Newcomb, T. M., 'Some Attitudinal Effects of Experimentally Increased Salience of a Membership Group', in *Readings in Social Psychology* (third ed.), ed. Maccoby, E. E., Newcomb, T. M. and Hartley, E. L., London: Methuen & Co. Ltd., 1958.

Cooper, E. and Jahoda, M., 'The Evasion of Propaganda: How Prejudiced People Respond to Anti-prejudice Propaganda' *Journal of Psychology*, 23, 15–25, 1947.

Crespi, L., 'The Influence of Military Government Sponsorship in German Opinion Polling', *Internat. J. Opin. Attit. Res.* IV, 151, 1950.

Drever, J., A *Dictionary of Psychology*, Penguin Books, 1952.

Guest, L. L., 'A Study of Interviewer Competence', *Internat. J. Opin. Attit. Res.*, I, No. 4, 17–30, 1947.

Hildum, D. C. and Brown, R. W., 'Verbal Reinforcement and Interviewer Bias', *J. Abnorm. Soc. Psy.* 3, 283–296, 1956.

Hyman, H. H. et al, *Interviewing in Social Research*, Univ. of Chicago Press, 1954.

Jung, C. G., *Modern Man in Search of a Soul*, London: Routledge and Kegan Paul, 1933.

Kahn, R. L. and Cannell, C. F., *The Dynamics of Interviewing*, N.Y.: Wiley, 1957.

Katz, D., 'Do Interviewers Bias Poll Results?' *Pub. Opin. Quart.* 6, 248–268, 1942.

Kelley, H. H., 'Salience of Membership and Resistance to Change of Group Anchored Attitudes', *Hum. Rel.* 8, 275–289, 1955.

Krech, D. and Crutchfield, R. S., *Theory and Problems of Social Psychology*, N.Y.: McGraw-Hill, 1948.

Maier, N. R. F., *Psychology in Industry*, London: Harrap, 1955.

Mead, M., *Coming of Age in Samoa*, N.Y.: Morrow & Co. Inc., 1928.

Mead, M., *Growing up in New Guinea*. N.Y.: Morrow & Co. Inc., 1930.

Newcomb, T. M. and Svehla, G., 'Intra-family Relationship in Attitude', *Sociometry*, I, 180–205, 1937.

Psychotherapy, I, No. 3, 1965.

Rice, S., 'Contagious Bias in the Interview: a Methodological Note', *Amer. J. Soc.* 35, 420–423, 1929.

Roethlisberger, F. J. and Dickson, W. J., *Management and the Worker*, Harvard Univ. Press, 1943.

Sanford, R. N., *Psychology of Personality*, J. L. McCory (ed.), 305–312, Logos Press, USA, 1959.

Sidney, E. and Brown, M., *The Skills of Interviewing*, London: Tavistock Publications, 1961.

Problem-solving Interviews

Smith, H. L. and Hyman, H., 'The Biasing Effect of Interviewer Expectations on Survey Results', *Pub. Opin. Quart.* 14, 491–506, 1950.

Sorenson, O., *The Observed Changes Enquiry*, N.Y.: G.E.C., 1958.

Watson, W. S. and Hartmann, G. W., 'The Rigidity of a Basic Attitudinal Frame', *J. Abnorm. Soc. Psy.* 34, 314–335, 1959.

INDEX

121